Andrew P. Peabody

Christianity the Religion of Nature

lectures delivered before the Lowell Institute. Second Edition

Andrew P. Peabody

Christianity the Religion of Nature
lectures delivered before the Lowell Institute. Second Edition

ISBN/EAN: 9783337262884

Printed in Europe, USA, Canada, Australia, Japan

Cover: Foto ©Lupo / pixelio.de

More available books at **www.hansebooks.com**

CHRISTIANITY

THE

RELIGION OF NATURE.

LECTURES

DELIVERED BEFORE THE LOWELL INSTITUTE

BY

A. P. PEABODY, D. D., LL.D.,

PREACHER TO THE UNIVERSITY, AND PLUMMER PROFESSOR OF CHRISTIAN MORALS
IN HARVARD COLLEGE.

Second Edition, Revised.

BOSTON:
GOULD AND LINCOLN,
59 WASHINGTON STREET.
NEW YORK: SHELDON AND COMPANY.
CINCINNATI: GEORGE S. BLANCHARD.
1870.

PREFACE.

THE author by no means claims as original the conception of Christianity as coincident with the religion of nature; but he is not aware that precisely this line of proof or defence has been adopted in any formal treatise on the evidences of Christianity. Yet he is profoundly convinced that it is on grounds of *a priori* probability that the controversy between those who admit and those who deny a special, authoritative revelation through Jesus Christ is now to be waged.

It is not a little singular that *a priori* objections took precedence of historical in the early days of the Church. We have no reason to suppose that Celsus denied the miraculous element in the Evangelical narratives. In times of ready faith as to the occult and marvellous in nature and the wonder-working power of demons, it was easy to admit the salient facts recorded in the Gospels, and yet to reject the truths which they seemed to authenticate. The two leading considerations urged by Celsus against the new religion were its promulgation among and for the poor, uneducated, and ignoble, and its claim to universality, both which features appeared to him so intrinsically absurd as to be incapable of proof. It is no mean evidence of the penetrating and transforming power of the religion thus assailed, that these strongest points of attack are now impregnable stations of defence, — that the whole civilized world would demand as essentials of a divinely authenticated religion that it should embrace within its blessings and its promises all sorts and conditions of men, and that it should be adapted to universal acceptance.

In the last century, Hume indeed maintained the antecedent impossibility of miracles in such a sense as to render them incapable of being authenticated; it being, as he argued, more probable that any conceivable amount of human testimony should be false, than that they should be true. But the greater part of the infidel writers of the century aimed their attacks at the alleged facts and the historical evidences of the Hebrew and Christian Scriptures. Accordingly, it was the prime object of the advocates of Christianity to accumulate proofs of the genuineness and authenticity of the sacred writings. This they did, some of them with more zeal and thoroughness than discrimination and critical discernment. *Non multum, sed multa*, might well have been the motto of not a few, and testimonies of unimpeachable validity and explicitness were often weakened by their juxtaposition with those of doubtful authority or of imperfect relevancy. Lardner's great work lies especially open to this objection, if we consider it as an argument for Christianity, while as a repertory of the materials for argument it cannot be too highly prized or too gratefully regarded. Paley's treatise on the E dences of Christianity, on the other hand, was admirably adapted to the exigencies of his time. It seems to us a complete refutation of historical scepticism. It is not obsolete, and never can become so. In our own day, with a narrower scope, Mr. Norton's great work on the Genuineness of the Gospels is unequalled as a compact array of historical arguments. His motto is, *Non multa, sed multum.* He rejects all testimony against which a shadow of doubt or a charge of irrelevancy can be urged, nay, almost all individual testimony; for the witnesses that he places on the stand are, with hardly an exception, communities or bodies of men, and official personages who must have virtually spoken in the name and expressed the belief of the several churches or the collective Christendom which they represented. The second and third volumes, comprising the history of the various Gnostic sects, evince conclusively that those heretics, who on theological grounds could not but have rejoiced to invalidate our canonical Gospels, could find no historical pretence for their rejection. Mr. Norton also, at several points, adduces the strongest circumstantial evidence for these Gospels, showing that certain universally admitted states of belief and ecclesiastical habitudes could not have existed, had not the genuineness of the Gospels been universally regarded as beyond dispute. In fine, writers of this historical school have proved conclusively that the authorship of the four Gospels, the Acts of the Apostles, and the Epistles of St. Paul, by the men whose names they bear, rests on much stronger evidence than can be adduced for the genuineness of any other writings of equal antiquity; and that the facts which they record or recognize have all, and more than all, the marks of authenticity which belong to the universally admitted facts of ancient history.

It may indeed be said that the now dominant school of infidelity, naturalism, or pseudo-Christianity stands on the high ground of searching historical criticism. This we deny. Its historical conclusions are not reasons for, but corollaries from, its unbelief. It assumes the *a priori* impossibility of revelation, special inspiration, and miracle, and on that basis erects its theories of the genesis of the sacred books and of the (so-called) legends or myths which they record. Their reasoning is this: "Had the actual companions of Jesus Christ written the Gospels, their contents could not have been so utterly false as we know them to be; therefore these books were of later date, of divided authorship, of gradual growth." Were the critical canons and processes of Strauss and the Tübingen divines applied to any other than our sacred books, the manifest result would be a *reductio ad absurdum*. Were these canons and processes admitted in any other field of historical or bibliographical research, no ancient book whatever could be received as genuine, no fact a few centuries old could be regarded as otherwise than fabulous or doubtful, and the whole realm of the past would be given over to Pyrrhonism. But the desperate expedients to which writers of this school are driven, may be regarded as furnishing a valuable contribution to the Christian evidences. Their problem is to account for the existence, internal character, and general reception of the Gospels on the hypothesis that their contents are in the main false. They can solve this problem only by maintaining that these books came into being and grew into their present shape in ways in which no books were ever known to have their birth and growth ; and that — mere foundlings, the children of many parents, owned of none — they foisted themselves at once, as of apostolic authority, upon the faith and reverence of Christian communities in every part of the civilized world. A problem which admits of no more rational solution than this is unsolvable.

Meanwhile the phasis of scepticism which now so extensively prevails renders it incumbent on Christians to demonstrate that the religion of the Gospel is in all its parts, in all its apparatus, in all its history, natural religion, — that it is not a provisional scheme, not a supplementary dispensation, but co-eternal with the mind of God, and coeval with the souls of men, — that its doctrines and precepts are not true and right because they were revealed, but that they were revealed because they are essentially true and immutably right. It is only when this conviction is produced in the mind of the objector, that he is prepared to listen to argument and to weigh evidence as to the historical aspects of the question.

The following Lectures grew out of an invitation received by the author, to prepare for the Lowell Institute a course of Lectures on Natural Religion. He, regarding Christianity as natural religion *par excellence*, asked and obtained permission to fill out a programme for the prescribed course arranged in accordance with this view. As a treatise this volume is incomplete, and less nearly complete than it might have seemed had a single province of the large field of inquiry been selected. But the author deemed it advisable, in a series of public Lectures, rather to illustrate the extended application of his mode of reasoning, than to attempt the thorough treatment of any one department of the subject to the neglect of all the rest.

The author has in several instances incorporated in these Lectures passages of his own articles previously printed in the periodicals to which he has been a frequent contributor. He has not thought it expedient, or even right, to omit things that needed to be said, because he had said them elsewhere, or to present in a meaner guise thoughts which he had once arrayed in the best attire he could weave for them.

The work is offered to the public, not without sincere diffidence as to its merits, but with an assurance which cannot be made stronger, that the citadel of our faith is for the present to be maintained and defended chiefly on such grounds as are here exhibited.

HARVARD UNIVERSITY, October 15, 1863.

CONTENTS.

LECTURE I.

NATURAL AND REVEALED RELIGION.

	PAGE
Christianity as old as the Creation	13
Religion defined	17
Distinction between Natural and Revealed Religion	19
Alleged Sources of Religious Knowledge, — Consciousness	19
Intuition	21
Reasoning	23
Analogy proves nothing	24
Office of Analogy	26
Amount of Religious Knowledge attainable independently of Revelation	28
Imperfections of Natural Religion	29

LECTURE II.

REVELATION.

Revelation defined	32
Natural Religion the Material for Revelation	33
Revelation a Postulate of Human Nature	34
Demanded by the Analogy of the Divine Government	36
Rendered probable by the Nature of God	38
Objections to Christianity grounded on its late Promulgation and limited Diffusion	42
Fitness of the Christian Era for the Establishment of Christianity	45

LECTURE III.

MIRACLES.

Revelation needs to be authenticated	51
Belief in Miracles natural to Man	56
Miracles, a part of the Course of Nature	58
Not necessarily Exceptions to Natural Laws	65
Worth of a miraculously attested Revelation, in Temptation . . .	67
In Sorrow . . .	68

LECTURE IV.

RECORDS OF REVELATION.

Man's Need of Authoritative Scriptures	72
Revelation must needs create its own Literature	75
Marks of Authenticity in the Hebrew and Christian Scriptures . .	76
Human Element in the Scriptures	83
Tokens of the Divine Element in their Authorship	88

LECTURE V.

THE LOVE OF GOD.

Man may verify what he could not discover	93
Beneficent Ends in Nature	95
The Natural Theology of Pain	98
Moral Evil	102
The Paternal Providence of God	104
The Case of the Unprivileged	109

LECTURE VI.

THE PROVIDENCE OF GOD IN HUMAN ART.

Art is but the Use or Imitation of Nature	116
Adaptation of Man's Physical Constitution to the Purposes of Art .	123
All Art Mathematical	130

LECTURE VII.

THE PROVIDENCE OF GOD IN HUMAN SOCIETY.

The Solidarity of the Human Family a Christian Idea	134
Mutual Relations of the Races	135
Distribution of Natural Endowments	139
The Laboring Classes not cut off from the Means of Improvement	145
Man overworked	147
What Machinery will do for the Laborer	151

LECTURE VIII.

THE HOLINESS OF GOD.—GOD IN CHRIST.

God's Holiness manifested in the Human Conscience	156
In his Retributive Providence	162
Accordance with Nature of Christ's Mediatorial Office	164
Of his Manifestation of the Divine Attributes	165
Of his Moral Perfectness	168
Of his outward Condition and Experiences	171

LECTURE IX.

IMMORTALITY.

The Soul Immaterial, and therefore Immortal	176
Perception the Function of the Soul	180
Immortality inferred from the Changes that take place in Life	183
From the Phenomena of Death	184
Arguments for Immortality from Man's Intellectual and Moral Nature	186
From the Growth of Character in Old Age	189
From the Waste of Life	191
From the Instinct of Self-Advancement	193

LECTURE X.

CHRISTIAN MORALITY.

Christian Morality universal and eternal	196
The Mutual Dependence of Piety and Charity original in the Gospel	199

The Pietistic Element divorced from the Philanthropic 201
Philanthropy without Piety 204
The two united in Christ and in Christianity 206
The Reconciliation of Self-Love and Brotherly Love peculiar to the
    Gospel 209

LECTURE XI.

THE NATURAL RELIGION OF THE STATE.

The Family the Germ of the State 216
The Fifth Commandment of the Decalogue a Political Precept . . 217
Relation of Domestic Life to State Life 221
Civilization, its Means and its Hinderances 227
Christianity essential to Progressive Civilization 232
Contrast between Ancient and Modern Civilization 235

LECTURE XII.

THE SABBATH A LAW OF NATURAL RELIGION. — CONCLUSION.

Christian Institutions 237
The Sabbath primeval 239
    A law of the Human Body and of the Material Universe . 242
    Essential to Intellectual Growth and Vigor . . . 244
    A Civilizing Agent 246
    Conduces to Man's Political Well-being 248
    Indispensable to the Religious Nature 251
Recapitulation of the Course 254
Comparative Worth of the Internal and External Evidences of Chris-
    tianity 255
Conclusion 256

CHRISTIANITY

THE RELIGION OF NATURE.

LECTURE I.

NATURAL AND REVEALED RELIGION.

THERE stands an ancient architectural pile, with tokens of its venerable age covering it from its corner-stone to its topmost turret; and some imagine these to be tokens of decay, while to others they only indicate, by the years they chronicle, a massiveness that can yet defy more centuries than it has weathered years. Its foundation is buried in the accumulated mould and clustered mosses of many generations. Its walls are mantled and hidden by parasitic vines. Its apartments are some of them dank and cold, as if their very cement were dissolving in chilly vapors. Others, built against the walls, were never framed into them; and now their ceilings are broken, their floors are uneven as the surface of a billow, their timbers seem less to sustain one another than to break one another's fall. All through the house you see dilapidated furniture, — ornaments so called, which lost their last touch of gilding and trace of beauty ages ago, — articles once of use, which it seems absurd to call utensils now, so entirely has their need gone by and their purpose become effete. There are dwellers in the mansion whose whole demeanor makes you tremble lest the structure fall on your head or collapse beneath your feet. They will not have a cobweb disturbed, lest the ceiling should crumble at the touch of the broom. They are afraid to move the furniture, lest there be found some ugly gap in the wall behind. And as for righting any of the displaced beams, or substituting new timbers where the old are thoroughly worm-eaten, they would as soon consent to have the whole building undermined or blown up. They assure you that it is still safe and strong, wind-proof and storm-proof, and that they want no other dwelling till its builder and owner shall prepare for them a new mansion under a brighter sky and in a more genial climate. But the very tones in which they give you this assurance are so hesitating, and they move about with so soft and cat-like a tread, and look so much alarmed at the least gust of wind, you can hardly persuade yourself that they believe what they say.

You determine, therefore, to make your own investigations. You dig away the mould, and lo! the foundation was laid by no mortal hand; it is primitive rock that strikes its roots down an unfathomable depth into the solid earth, so that no frosts can heave it, no convulsions shake it. You tear the ivy from the walls, and you find them built of Cyclopean stones tongued and grooved into each other, betraying a power and skill that have no counterpart in the masonry of these modern times, and not a stone can need readjusting while the world shall stand. In every buttress and cross-wall, in the jointed slabs that constitute the roof and the Atlantean pillars that sustain it, you discern, with the unspent strength of ages past, hoarded strength for unnumbered ages to come.

As to the feeble, tottering, effete portions of the edifice and its contents, you ascertain that all which bears the marks of decay is of comparatively recent date, — floors and partitions extemporized to suit the whims of individual occupants, mere personal furniture, movables that do not belong there, — so that what seems old is new, while what is really old gives presage of perpetual youth.

Such an edifice is Christianity. The sceptic denies, the timid disciple doubts, its stability. The cry, "The Church is in danger," is almost as old as the Church; and there has never been a time when there has not been in some quarters a tendency to repress inquiry, to discourage thorough discussion, to distrust learning and science as forces that might shake the foundation of man's eternal hope. Even to the most friendly eye there is much about Christianity — not of it — of which we cannot say that it will last always, or wish that it may last long. It has extra-Scriptural technicalities of phrase and dogma which the world is happily outgrowing. Some of its rituals and organizations are fast losing their hold on the popular reverence. Its records are passing through the fierce ordeal of a scientific criticism, which may dislodge various old traditions as to their interpretation and office. Its partition-walls are in so crumbling a condition that they can hardly be propped up much longer, and through many of them bold breaches are already made, and strong hands are shaking and loosening the weak mortar and frail rafters of which they are built.

Yet Christianity none the less presents the aspect of impregnable strength, its foundation the Rock of Ages, its walls upheaved, its top-stone laid, by the hand that built the heavens, and spread the floor of the ocean, and reared the everlasting hills. Tindall's deistical work, "Christianity as old as the Creation, or the Gospel a Republication of the Law of Nature," admits in its title the strongest ground, nay, the only ground, on which we can believe or defend Christianity. To suppose it a Divine afterthought, a supplementary creation, an excrescence upon nature, is to dishonor it under shelter of pretended advocacy, — nay, more, it is to impugn the Divine immutableness, — the integrity of those attributes which underlie all religion. The highest view of Christianity is that which regards it as the religion of nature, as the constitutional law of the spiritual universe, as corresponding to the mathematical laws which are embodied in the material universe, — absolute, necessary, eternal truth, — that which always was and ever will be. Revelation did not create it, any more than Newton created the law of universal gravitation, or Kepler the laws of planetary motion. What Newton and Kepler were to the material universe, inspired men and the God-born Saviour were to the spiritual universe. Christianity was before the Word became flesh, before Moses, before Abraham; it will equally be when in the open vision of heaven the written Word shall be no longer needed.

This is the view which I propose to illustrate in the present course of Lectures. Natural Religion is the subject assigned to me. My purpose is to demonstrate the identity of Christianity with natural religion.

The residue of this Lecture will be occupied with the definition of the term *religion*, with the distinction ordinarily made between natural and revealed religion, and with the sources and contents of natural religion as distinguished from revealed.

As to the meaning of *religion*, its derivation gives us but doubtful and imperfect guidance. I should prefer, in common with almost all grammarians and lexicographers, ancient and modern, to derive it from *religare*, to *rebind*, that is, to bind anew, and with new tenacity, the human spirit to its Author and Father. But Cicero, who understood his language better than we do, and whose authority on such a point one hardly dares to disavow, says that *religio* comes from *relegere*, to *reperuse*, that is, to ponder seriously and intently, and that those who gave their earnest heed to things relating to the gods were called *religious* [*religiosi*], *ex relegendo*.[1] According to the first of these derivations, religion is the science of our relations and obligations; according to the second, it is the science of the things which lie beneath the surface and are taken note of only by the heedful, that is, of things unseen and spiritual; — two definitions which, widely as they differ in their terms, coincide as to their contents. We might comprehend the two in one, and define religion to be the science of our unseen, or rather our supersensual relations. When we discriminate between the religion of the intellect and that of the heart, we denote by the former a belief in those relations, by the latter a state of character in accordance with that belief. There are two or three comments to be made on this definition before proceeding farther.

1. There is a religion. There are supersensual truths and facts. Even to deny the being of God or the existence of the human soul, is not to eliminate religion from the circle of the sciences. Being has its cause, its laws; there are reasons for the existence of things as they are; and this cause, these laws, these reasons, are religion.

[1] De Natura Deorum, II. 28.

The theory which substitutes for the sublime genealogy of Holy Writ, with its anthem-like close, " which was the son of Adam, which was the son of God," the descent, or rather the ascent, of man from the animalcule, the tadpole, the prone quadruped, the ape, if true, is religion, — it defines our unseen relations.

2. There is but one religion. It is, in the nature of things, impossible that there should be more than one. If any specific proposition or set of propositions with reference to our unseen relations be true, any other proposition or set of propositions covering the same ground must be false. If Christianity be true, it is not *a religion*, as it is sometimes called, but *religion*. If Judaism also be true, it is so, not as distinct from, but as coincident with, Christianity, — the one religion, to which it can bear only the relation borne by the part to the whole. If there be portions of truth in other religious systems, they are not portions of other religions, but portions of the one religion, which somehow became incorporated with fables and falsities.

3. This one religion, whatever it be, is cognizable by the human mind. I do not mean that all supersensual truth is thus cognizable. There are undoubtedly aspects in which the Divine character is beyond our conception. Nay, the mode of our own being and the laws of finite existence in general are attainable by us only in part. But our relations we are capable of knowing. What God is to us, and what we are to him, we are competent to understand. Our relations to one another, our obligations, our accountability, our destiny, — whether it be annihilation or continued existence after death, — are also subjects of our possible knowledge. Let it not be said that the themes of religious speculation are infinite, and

therefore incomprehensible. We admit that the Infinite as such cannot be comprehended by a finite mind; but the finite acts and manifestations of the Infinite, so far from being incomprehensible, constitute in the last analysis all our knowledge.

We come now to the distinction between natural and revealed religion. These terms designate, not different classes of truths, but the different methods in which religious truth becomes known to mankind. What is ascertained by the unaided exercise of man's own powers is called natural religion; what is received on testimony is called revealed religion. But the latter is no less natural than the former. The fatherhood of God, the forgiveness of sins, mediation, atonement, retribution, if truths, are truths of Divine and human nature, essential, everlasting truths, no less so because unknown, formerly to all, and still to the greater part of mankind, than if man were born to the knowledge of them. The Bible, indeed, recognizes the validity of this statement. Its Gospel is "the everlasting Gospel." Its promises are "the eternal purpose of God." Its redemption sacrifice is "the Lamb slain from the foundation of the world."

Our first inquiry in the department of natural religion is as to the sufficiency of man's unaided powers to arrive at a knowledge of religious truth. If this knowledge be attained, it must be attained either by consciousness, by intuition, or by reasoning. Let us consider successively these alleged sources of religious knowledge.

I. Consciousness. We are conscious only of ourselves, — of our own conditions of thought and feeling. Consciousness gives us no knowledge of anything outside of ourselves, — no objective knowledge. I am not conscious of these lights, these faces, but only of certain impressions on my visual organs, which I know, on grounds independent of my consciousness, must proceed from gas-lights and human countenances. I am not conscious of the existence of my friend. I am conscious merely of my affection for him, and of my own assurance that the affection is reciprocated. His existence and his regard for me I have learned through other sources. I am not conscious of the being and attributes of God. I cannot be conscious of his providence or of his love to me. My own consciousness can teach me nothing concerning his consciousness. I am conscious of the capacity of reverence, but not of its object, — of the conception of infinity, but not of the Infinite Being. When I learn from sources independent of my consciousness that God is, and that he does good continually, I am conscious of love and gratitude to him.

Again, consciousness is of the present moment, not of the past or the future. I am not conscious of what I said and did yesterday. I am conscious of certain remembrances; but those remembrances, though of the past, constitute my present state of mind, — the past, when it loses its hold on my memory, drops out of my consciousness. Equally little can I be conscious of the future. I may be conscious of hopes more or less well-grounded; but I am full as vividly conscious, often, of fallacious hopes, as of hopes that are to be realized. I am not conscious of immortality. I may be conscious of adaptation, desire, longing for continued existence; but this consciousness is no more the evidence of its own realization, than my consciousness of adaptation, desire, longing for some office or emolument that in no wise depends on myself, is evidence of its own realization. I am, indeed, conscious of tastes, loves, joys, aspirations, which are independent of my material organization, and which *may* outlast it, — I therefore am not conscious that I shall wholly die when the body dies. But equally little am I conscious that I shall necessarily survive the body. On the other hand, my being is not necessary. I began to be. A few years ago I was not. It is no more necessary that I should be a century hence, than that I should have been a century ago.

Consciousness, then, is not an adequate source of religious knowledge.

II. How is it with intuition? Intuition is spontaneous belief, — the perception of the intellect. There are truths which we discern without reasoning, and which cannot be demonstrated by reasoning. Thus we know, but cannot prove, that a part is less than the whole; that a straight line is the shortest distance between two points; that, if equal quantities be taken from equal quantities, the remainders will be equal. In like manner we know, but cannot prove, that an effect implies a cause; that what is true of a species is true of the individuals that compose it; that the universal experience and testimony of mankind are a valid ground of belief. Truths of this class are necessarily developed with the development of the mind; they are a part of the mental organism; they are wanting only in the infant, the idiot, and the undeveloped savage. No sane mind that has attained to self-reflection denies or doubts them. Now even the most simple religious truths are obviously not of this class. There have been well-developed and highly-cultivated minds that have believed in no god and in many gods, that have rejected personal immortality, that have acquiesced in the most grovelling materialism.

Nay, among the philosophical thinkers and writers who profess to regard intuition as the prime source of our supersensual knowledge, a very large proportion at the present moment are pantheists, and maintain that the human soul at death lapses from self-consciousness, and is reabsorbed into the impersonal soul of the universe. On the other hand, those who think that they have an intuitive perception of God and of immortality are, with rare exceptions, persons who were nurtured under Christian auspices, whose earliest utterances were shaped in prayer, about whose infancy there hung a sacred atmosphere, and who drew in these sublime verities with the first rudiments of knowledge.

I confess that, were I to consult my own present consciousness, I might term the primal truths of religion intuitive; for I am sure that with me they depend not on reasoning or testimony, nor could any possible weight of argument disprove them. But then those truths are inseparable in my thought from a Christian mother's teachings, and from the dying benediction which is all that I remember of a sainted father; and there are other collateral beliefs which I know to be questionable, yet which I can never question, — which are to me equally like intuitions, because they came to me through the same hallowed medium. And when I reflect on the countless multitude of keen, clear-sighted men who have lived and died in ignorance of the one God and the life eternal, and on the less numerous, yet by no means feeble, host of vigorous minds that have seen and spurned the full light of evangelic teaching on these same truths, have denied their God, and have embraced annihilation as their certain destiny, I cannot regard the truths of religion as necessary or intuitive beliefs.

III. There remains to be considered reasoning as a source of religious knowledge. The proper province of reasoning is to perform for our knowledge or belief precisely the office which chemistry performs for material substances, that of analysis or decomposition. It ascertains the contents, the component parts, of what we previously knew or believed. A conclusion, in order to be valid, must be contained in its premises. But as to religious truth, our premises are but few and scanty; for what underived data for our reasoning as to themes which exceed the universe and embrace twin eternities can lie within the observation and experience of us, the children of yesterday and the dust?

Is it contended, however, that induction may transcend the bounds of observation and experience, — may infer general laws from the repetition of phenomena, universal truths from the aggregation of particular facts? I answer, that induction has a religious basis, presupposes a fundamental truth of religion, and therefore cannot be employed to establish that on which alone it depends. Induction is syllogism with the immutable attributes of God for a constant term. It is a mode of reasoning which, though so obviously valid to *our* conceptions, never entered into the logic of Pagan antiquity. It is entirely the growth of Christian culture, — of minds bathed in the Christian doctrine of a universal and perfect, harmonious and self-consistent Providence.

Very nearly the same statement applies to the argument from analogy. This too rests on the immutableness of the Divine attributes. On no other ground can we infer, where observation and experience do not reach, the extension of the laws and the embodiment of the principles which we trace and verify within the range open to our inspection. Analogy, therefore, like induction, presupposes the foundation-truths of religion, and cannot be employed to establish them. Indeed, induction and analogy coincide entirely with syllogism in this, — that the conclusion is contained in the premises. When we infer a general law, or an analogous fact, truth, or system, we simply announce what is included in the Divine immutableness which constitutes the major premiss, and the observed or known fact, or bundle of facts, which constitutes the minor premiss.

Moreover, analogy, thus defined, proves nothing. At the most, it establishes a strong probability, but never without some opening for doubt. Analogy is resemblance between objects of different classes, or between different departments of knowledge. When up to a certain point we trace a resemblance between two classes or departments, we infer that the resemblance extends to other points in which we cannot trace it. But it is always possible that at any one of these points resemblance ceases and difference begins.

Let us take for an instance the immortality of the soul. Among the many arguments for immortality derived from analogy, the following seems to me to be the strongest. To every order of organized and sentient beings, except man, there is open a sphere of development and action commensurate with its capacities. Analogy leads us to believe that man too has such a sphere. But he has it not in this world. Here there is so utter a disparity as to be ludicrous, were it not unspeakably sad, between his vast capacities and desires on the one hand, and his narrow stage and brief span of being on the other. There must then, we infer, be a life after death, which shall afford to man the scope for development which other animals find here. Every other terrestrial existence we can comprehend and round off in a cycle, all whose points lie within the sphere of our vision. Man is not complete within such a cycle. His being, therefore, if in analogy with that of his fellow-creatures, must reach on beyond death, and if beyond death, why not forever? To regard death as the extinction of his being makes his existence a solitary phenomenon, to which nothing in the entire universe corresponds. This reasoning has indeed a high probability in its favor, yet it falls far short of certainty; for man differs from all other sentient beings so widely, and in so many particulars, as to render it at least possible that this very incompleteness of his existence may be one of the points of difference.

Again, analogy often points equally to two opposite conclusions. Thus, on this very subject of immortality, how many hopeful analogies can we cite, — in the caterpillar whose death is but a new and higher birth, — in the grain of wheat reappearing in the sheaf, — in the annual resurrection-fiat that restores the winter's desolation, and renders back to tree and shrub a life which had seemed extinct, yet never was more vigorous than when it gave no sign! When in our happy and hopeful hours we throw out our unbuttressed arch of dreamy speculation toward heaven, these seem more than mere poetic fancies; they become symbols, prophecies, pledges of the life eternal. But when the shadow of death falls heavily around us; when those go from us who carry with them a solid portion of our own being; when we count the rapidly stealing years, and feel that our noon has passed, and we are gliding down the western slope of our brief day; when the fingers of disease are fumbling at our heart-strings, — then a troop of sad analogies force themselves upon us. We think of the blighted buds and germs, immeasurably more numerous than the fructifying, of the destruction with no resurrection in many departments of organized being, of the loss of identity in so many cases where there is a continuity of life; and these resemblances are melancholy presages of victorious death and a devouring grave. In fine, there is no form of belief, no hope, no fear, which may not fortify itself by analogies. Analogy, therefore, proves nothing, and cannot be a trustworthy source of religious knowledge.

What, then, is the office of analogy? It serves, in the first place, to guide us in the investigation of truth, and, secondly, to answer objections.

1. To guide us in the investigation of truth. The mere wish to discern truth is fruitless. Nature has but two answers — yes and no — for her inquirer; and whether he ever gets a yes, depends entirely on his skill in shaping his questions. What shall we ask? How shall we direct our inquiries in an unexplored field? Analogy must frame our questions, must suggest what we may reasonably expect to find. The likeness of things known and familiar may occur in things new and unexplored, and it is for this likeness that we are to look and ask, seeking, in what is as yet unknown, facts, principles, and laws analogous to those with which we are already conversant. Analogy thus carries the torch before us through the dim aisles of the temple of truth.

2. The second office of analogy is to remove objections which we cannot answer, against facts or truths in whose behalf we have a competent weight of positive evidence Of course, to answer objections is the readiest way of

removing them. But often, from their very nature, or from the finiteness of our knowledge, they do not admit of being answered. In this case they are adequately met, if we can show that similar and equal objections lie against facts or truths which all men regard as absolutely certain. Thus against the evangelic history infidels urge some objections which we must admit to be unanswerable; but if we can show that precisely the same objections lie against portions of history which no sane man denies or doubts, analogy proves these objections utterly futile and nugatory, even though they be unanswerable. For instance, in the book entitled "Historic Doubts relative to Napoleon Bonaparte," Archbishop Whately, with consummate skill and yet with transparent fairness and honesty, applies to the several Memoirs of Napoleon and Histories of his times precisely the principles on which Hume and infidels of his school had impugned the authenticity of the Gospels; and on those principles he proves that there is not a leading fact of Napoleon's life which does not admit of the gravest doubt, and yet more, that in all probability no such man as Napoleon ever existed. Now, as this line of argument could shake no man's belief in Napoleon's existence and history, reasoning from analogy, we conclude that the same line of argument has no validity against the Gospels.

We have a masterly specimen of this use of the argument from analogy in the fifteenth chapter of St. Paul's First Epistle to the Corinthians. He, first, from the resurrection of Christ proves that of all men, shows that Jesus rose expressly as the type and pledge of universal immortality, and rests the whole positive stress of his reasoning on this glorious fact, attested by a cloud of witnesses, most of whom were living when he wrote. But then comes the sceptical inquiry, "How can these things be? How are the dead raised, and with what bodies?" In reply, he exhibits in the outward universe instances of the resurrection of virtually the same body in a different form, as in the case of the kernel of wheat, which, without losing its identity, reappears in a guise unlike that in which it was thrown into the ground. By this analogy he shows that there is in the annual course of nature a similar fact, known and read of all men, multiplied myriads of times, in itself equally strange with the resurrection of the dead, and encompassed by the same difficulties.

Such are the alleged sources of natural religion, — consciousness, which cannot transcend self; intuition, which, strictly speaking, does not extend to religious truth; reasoning, which analyzes the previous items of our knowledge without adding to them.

How much may be derived from these doubtful and precarious sources? As regards the Divine Being, man could hardly fail to reach a belief in intelligence and power higher than his own. Nature bears unnumbered marks of design, and design implies a designer; while the immense forces whose equilibrium or conflict works out each successive form and stage of design in nature lead irresistibly to the attributing of vast power, conjoined with skill and wisdom, to the designing mind or minds. But here the argument from design ceases. It does not prove an infinite creator; for the universe is finite, and may have had a finite author. It does not prove the moral attributes of the Creator; for the agencies of nature lend their force to mischief and evil, — they are charged to execute the malicious purposes of the wicked, — they are fraught with ministries of woe to the wretched.

Yet more, the argument from design does not establish the unity or the personality of God. The harmony of nature is not readily perceived. Objects appear in isolated groups; events in isolated cycles. There is war among the elements. The sun ripens, the swollen river devastates, the harvest-field. The rain fills, the hot breath of summer dries, the fountain and the lake. Nature seems a vast battle-ground between opposing designs and antagonistic forces. Hence the human mind, constrained to believe in the existence of superhuman wisdom and power, resorts to polytheism, and cantons out the creation into separate provinces, each with its tutelar divinity.

Polytheism is the earliest stage of natural theology. With the progress of knowledge philosophy has birth. Contemplative minds awake to a sense of pervading system and order in the material universe. At this point speculation takes one of two directions. It either, still impressed with the perpetual conflict of good and evil, happiness and misery, in the world, resorts to the Oriental dualism, and conceives of a supremely good and a supremely evil principle, who share the sovereignty of the universe; or else, as in the Greek philosophy, it blends inseparably the shaping and benignant spirit with the brute and resisting matter through which it struggles for an ever more complete and full manifestation of itself, and thus frames an essentially pantheistic theology. There is reason to doubt whether natural religion, where the light of revelation has not preceded it, has ever transcended these forms of belief; and it is a significant fact, that in the present age the philosophy which ignores revelation constantly tends to return to pantheism, so that in the speculations of many of the profoundest thinkers of the eighteenth and nineteenth centuries the idea of a personal God, the object of reverence, worship, and prayer, is wholly eliminated, — nature is God, man is God become self-conscious, everything is God, and God is everything or — nothing.

As regards a future life, by virtue of intense longings, lame analogies, and inconclusive reasonings, natural religion attains to the conjecture, the strong hope of a continued existence; but in no instance has it reached a confidence sufficient for consolation in the severest stress of need, or adequate to furnish rules and motives for the conduct of life. Indeed, Cicero, in his attempt to prove immortality, is careful to show that, if his reasoning is faulty, annihilation is no great evil;[1] and when his daughter dies, he confesses that he has lost all faith in his own arguments.[2] Nay, the strongest argument for immortality that has come down to us from the ancient world is based on the assumption of the past eternity of the human soul, and may be compressed into the simple formula, — "That which had no beginning can have no end."[3]

As to the duties growing out of man's relations to God and his fellow-beings, they are derived in part from the essential conditions of life and of society, so that they could not remain wholly unknown; while, on the other hand, the comprehension of their entire extent and their mutual interdependence can result only from those clear and adequate conceptions of religious truth which cannot be reached by man's unaided powers. Accordingly, while the ancients promulgated many sound moral precepts, there is hardly one of them who has not impressed his sanction on some atrocious immorality. Even the divine Plato recommends the murder of feeble and sickly infants, expressly allows drunkenness at the feasts of Bac-

[1] Tusc. Quæst. I. 5-8. [2] Ep. ad Atticum, XII. 14.
[3] Plato's Phædo, 47-58.

chus, and authorizes some of the worst forms of licentiousness.

I admit that modern deists have in numerous instances maintained a pure and lofty personal monotheism, have expressed firm faith in immortality, and have inculcated and practised the severest morality. But I cannot forget that they were educated as Christians, and their subsequent unbelief could not shut out the light that came to them from the Sun of righteousness. To determine the utmost amount of religious truth that man can attain independently of revelation, we must interrogate minds that can have derived nothing from revelation. And we certainly cannot err in assuming that classic antiquity had reached the climax of extra-Christian culture. In all but their religious aspects the Greek and the Roman mind transcended the powers of the modern intellect, and have left us, in poetry, in history, in philosophy, and in some of the fine arts, models which we can emulate, but cannot equal, giving color, indeed, to the belief that the early ages possessed in mental force and acumen and in creative genius the same pre-eminence over modern times which we cannot but recognize in the physical proportions and strength of the ancients. But even Plato falls short of the clear conception of one personal Deity, and there hangs ever about his theology a pantheistic haze. Even Seneca, with an almost perfect system of ethics, fails to enter into the mystery of sorrow, cowers under the inevitable burdens and sufferings of humanity, and recommends that recourse to suicide which he illustrated by his own example. Even the dying Socrates, though he trusts that he is going to the society of good men, warns his friends not to be too confident in a matter attended by so much uncertainty.

LECTURE II.

REVELATION.

In my last Lecture, I considered the sources of religious knowledge which are open to man through the unaided exercise of his own powers. I propose this evening to illustrate the place and office of Revelation with reference to Natural Religion.

Revelation denotes *unveiling*,—*uncovering*. It implies the previous existence of that which is uncovered, or made known. It excludes the idea of newness, of invention, of recent creation. Watt *invented* the steam-engine, and Arkwright the spinning-jenny, which had no previous existence;—Galileo *revealed* the satellites of Jupiter, which are as old as the planet in its present form, and, according to the nebular hypothesis, older; Harvey *revealed* the circulation of the blood, which had been an unrevealed fact through all the antecedent ages of human history. Joseph Smith, his associates and successors, *created* what is peculiar to Mormonism; Mahomet *created* those portions of Mahometanism that he did not borrow, which are not truth, because they are the product of his own mind: we Christians believe that Jesus Christ *revealed* what is peculiar to Christianity, which is truth, because it was not the offspring of his own mind or age, but the disclosure of what was in the beginning in the mind of God, and in the nature, duty, and destiny of man.

We thus see that it is only natural religion which can furnish the material for revelation. The distinction between natural and revealed religion is not essential, but modal, — referring not to the substance, but to the means of our knowledge. The clown on the hill-top and the astronomer in his observatory see the same heavens; but where the former beholds only glittering points, the latter can trace the diversified disc of every planet, and can measure spaces and motions as if he trod the celestial paths with his chain and compass. In like manner, we can with the naked eye of reason and self-spun philosophy discern and know little of the spiritual universe, little even of our own nature, relations, and destiny; but when Christ puts the telescope to our eyes, and the measuring-rod in our hands, we can see and measure the things of which we had before been dimly cognizant or wholly ignorant. The revealed religion of the earth is the natural religion of heaven, — would be our natural religion, had we sufficiently comprehensive and penetrating minds to make it so, — will be our natural religion when the scales shall fall from our eyes in dying. Christianity, if true, is the fundamental law of spiritual being, as constant as the laws of nature, as unchangeable as the circuits of the stars. It is the physiology of the divine and the human spirit, the geography of the world of probation, duty, and accountability in which we live, the astronomy of those upper heavens where are the everlasting mansions of the redeemed. This physiology it is of immeasurable importance for man to know, that he may act worthily of his nature, — that he may not dwarf it, or debase it, or leave it undeveloped. This geography it profoundly concerns him to learn, that he may use the world as not abusing it.

With this astronomy it is for his highest interest and happiness that he become conversant, that from disappointment, and sorrow, and the death-shadow, when the whole lower firmament is darkened, he may lift his eyes to those unfading lights that burn around the eternal throne. But, as I showed you in my last Lecture, this is a department in which man has not at his own command the requisite means of research and sources of knowledge. I therefore maintain, that not only the contents of revelation, but the fact of revelation, belongs to natural religion; that is, that revelation is not only an historical fact, but a fact that was to have been anticipated on *a priori* grounds, — on grounds connected with the nature of man and of God.

I. For, first, revelation is a postulate of human nature. Its subjects are such as necessarily command the curiosity of the mind only a little raised above a mere animal existence. Religion comprises a department in which every thoughtful man perceives that there is something to be known, — real, objective truth. There comes up from the earliest ages that have left us their record the cry of the inquiring, longing soul, "O that I knew where I might find Him! Wherewith shall I approach Him, and how shall I order my ways before Him? If a man die, shall he live again?" And with this cry comes the thought of a revelation, as the only means by which it can be answered. The sense of this need found voice repeatedly among the philosophers of classic antiquity. Iamblichus, in describing the religious belief of Pythagoras and his followers, writes: "It is manifest that those things are to be done which are pleasing to God; but what they are it is not easy to know, except man were taught them by God himself, or by some person who had received them from God, or obtained the knowledge of them through some divine means."[1] There is a very striking passage in one of Plato's Dialogues, from which it would appear that he, or Socrates, in whose name he writes, anticipated a revelation as near at hand. Socrates meets one of his disciples going to a temple to pray, tries to convince him that he knows neither how to pray nor what to pray for, and then adds: "It seems best to me that we keep quiet. . . . . . It is absolutely necessary that we wait with patience, till we know certainly how we ought to behave toward God and man. . . . . . Till that time arrives, it may be safer to avoid offering sacrifices, of which you know not whether they are acceptable to God or not."[2] But the most remarkable passage of all is in the reply to his arguments for immortality put by Plato into the mouth of one of the disciples of Socrates: "I agree with you, Socrates, that to discover the certain truth of these things in this life is absolutely impossible, or at least very difficult. Yet not to inquire into what may be said about them, or to desist from our inquiry before we have carried it as far as possible, is the mark of a mean and low spirit. We ought, therefore, by all means to do one of these two things, — either by hearkening to instruction and by our own diligent study to find out the truth, or, if this be impossible, then to fix upon that which to human reason appears best and most probable, and to make this our raft, while we sail through life, unless we could have a more sure and safe conveyance, such as *some divine communication* would be."[3] Similar expressions might be

[1] Περὶ τοῦ Πυθαγορικοῦ βίου, Chap. 28.
[2] Second Alcibiades, 22, 23.
[3] Phædo, 78. λόγου θείου τινος.

multiplied, showing that the religion of nature is throughout an interrogative religion, which yearns for an answer to its questions from a more than human wisdom.

In accordance with this view, we find a universal appetency for revelation. Sacred books, oracles, prophets, have always been received with a ready faith. Christian missionaries, in earlier and later times, while they have often encountered insuperable obstacles, have left no record of antecedent scepticism as to the fact of a revelation. On the other hand, the very declaration that they were bearers of a divine message has in innumerable instances opened to its reception minds and hearts, which would have been stubbornly closed against such teachings as they might have promulgated on their own authority.

I know, indeed, that modern deists have disclaimed revelation as a postulate of the human soul. But why? Because they have enriched their naturalism with the spoils of Christianity. Were we carefully to explore a vast and curiously furnished subterranean chamber by the light of a torch, we might on a second visit discern the shape and size of every object by the few and straggling rays of light from the cave's mouth. But let another party enter for the first time without a torch, they would stumble at every step, and would be able to distinguish nothing by the same light by which we had seen everything. Modern deists in Christian countries had the light of the torch, before they deemed themselves independent of it. The ancients, groping from the first in darkness, longed for the torch, and despaired of finding their way without it.

II. There is antecedent reason in the nature of things to suppose that the postulate of the human soul for divine revelation would be satisfied. Unless the religious craving be an exception, there is no demand of man that has not its answer, no want that is not supplied, no yearning that does not find its response. Hunger levies contributions on every department of nature, and there is no zone or climate that yields not food fit for its inhabitants. For thirst there are springs even in the desert, and reservoirs in the arid rock. For man's social cravings, provision is made in the essential laws and conditions of birth and nurture, and in the necessities and mutual dependences of even the lowest types of savage life. For the still profounder need of loving and being loved, there is no relation between human beings which has not its instinctive and spontaneous action upon the emotional nature, so that in the whole commerce of domestic and social life there is a perpetual interweaving of more and more fine and delicate fibres of sympathy and fellow-feeling. The same correlation of demand and supply pervades the entire realm of science and knowledge. No class of objects or phenomena, however recondite, is presented to our curiosity, without means of ascertaining its nature, laws, sources, and causes. Among things observed and experienced no question is ever asked, and asked persistently, for which the answer is not lodged within the seeker's reach. How profound are the researches, how severely accurate the discoveries, constantly made as to objects that might seem too vast for comprehension, or too minute for cognizance, or too remote for precise measurement and analysis! We mark the perturbations of Uranus, detect the metallic particles in the atmosphere of the sun, trace organic life back to its infinitesimal type and outbudding. Meanwhile, here is our instinct of reverence, which has no definite object, — our inquiry into supersensual truth, which returns to us as void, as unsatisfied, as in the infancy of the race, — our earnest onlooking, before which hangs death, no less than ever a dense, impenetrable veil.

Not only are the soul's religious wants profound and intense, but mere mental progress and cultivation, so far from meeting them, only render them more utterly hopeless. Thus in the ruder days of Athens and Rome there was doubtless a sincere, and to a certain extent a satisfying, faith in the gods of the popular mythology and in the fables about Elysium; while with the growth of knowledge, religion on the one hand rationalized itself into pantheism, and on the other attenuated itself into atheism.

These religious wants of man, as I showed you in my last Lecture, are not susceptible of satisfaction through the agency of the human mind, with the instruments of inquiry that natively belong to it. But their very existence authorizes the assurance that they are satisfied somehow or somewhere. Now revelation is to the religious wants what food is to hunger, water to thirst, kindred to the loving heart, scientific truth to the inquiring intellect.

III. There is, also, in the nature of God antecedent reason to suppose that he would have made a revelation. I will for the present exclude from my argument those fatherly attributes of the Divine character, for which we are indebted, as I think, to revelation, and which, therefore, we cannot employ in proof of a revelation without reasoning in a circle. I will simply assume, what the marks of contrivance in the universe certainly demonstrate, creative design, that is, creative intelligence; and I will suppose that this intelligence belongs to a single divine mind, though my argument would remain unaffected on the hypothesis of dualism, or even of polytheism.

God made man, — made him not mere brute existence, but mind, soul, will, affection. He has made each human mind capable of communion with other created minds, so that it can take cognizance of their thoughts and emotions, and can receive from them knowledge, sentiment, and impulse. Is it conceivable that he should have shut out from himself the very avenues of communion which he has opened to created spirits, — that he should have put into the hands of his creatures keys with which they can unlock every chamber of intellect, fancy, and feeling, and can with intimate consciousness pervade, as it were, the whole of one another's inward being, — and that, as regards himself, he should have locked every door and thrown away the keys? The power to open every soul to the direct communion of every other soul includes and implies the power to open every soul to his own direct communion. The fact that he has thus established communion between soul and soul, renders it probable that he has also established communion between himself and the souls of men.

Still further, we can hardly conceive of God's having created intelligent minds, without the will to become himself an object of their intelligence, — to be distinctly recognized and known by them. So far is the idea of revelation from being unnatural, that any mode of communication would seem more natural than eternal silence. To my mind, while some of the early Scriptural narratives savor so much of anthropomorphism, that I cannot object to a somewhat free and allegorical interpretation of them, the literal sense — according to which the voice of the Almighty was heard in the garden in the cool of the day, was listened and replied to by the first-born among men, was made audible to the patriarch in his tent, and to Samuel in his bed hard by the ark of the covenant — has a naturalness, a reality, a lifelikeness, O, immeasurably greater than the heartless theory according to which the Creator has abandoned his offspring to perpetual orphanhood, has cut himself off forever from their conscious intercourse with him, has given them no authentic and incontrovertible tokens of his being, his nature, and their relation to him.

Again, man must have been created with some definite design or purpose on the part of the Creator, as to the development and exercise of his moral and active powers. It is impossible that God should not have a will as to the dispositions and deeds of his intelligent offspring, and laws which he would have them obey. On all the rest of creation he has impressed his will and law, and all things are obedient thereunto. Inanimate nature is bound by adamantine chains of immutable law. The fiat, "Hitherto shalt thou come, but no further," throbs in every pulse of air and ocean, in the waves of light and sound, in growth, vicissitude, catastrophe, and disintegration. Instinct in animals attends and attests design, and not one of them can transcend or fall short of his manifest place, office, and purpose in the universe. Man alone has an autonomic will, the power of choice between good and evil, between parallel courses of seeming good, between like, diverse, or opposite aims. Man alone is capable of obeying or disobeying law. And no one doubts that there are laws in obeying which he fulfils the purpose, works out the destiny, for which he was created. But he is capable of attaining to the knowledge of those laws only approximately and imperfectly. He had a fair opportunity and an open field, room for the trial of all kinds of moral experiments, ample time for ascertaining the right and the good, in the thousands of years that preceded the Christian era. He had all the lights of prolonged experience, profound philosophy, high and varied civilization. And with what results? As we have seen, there had been attained nothing that can now be regarded as a perfect system of ethics. There was no vice which had not its apologists, no virtue which had not its detractors, among the wisest and best men of their day. Nay, some essential virtues were not even recognized by name, or were regarded as tokens of imbecility. Moreover, if Jesus Christ was not a revealer of God's will, his system must be ranked among the most grossly vicious ethical systems of antiquity; for Christianity, if not a divine revelation, pretended to be one, was foisted in upon the world by a gigantic imposture, and therefore can never reckon veracity and honesty in its catalogue of virtues. Now it is incredible that an intelligent Creator should, with a definite design, have created a race of free moral agents, have made them incapable of ascertaining by the best exercise of their own powers what he would have them do and abstain from, and yet at no time and in no way have given them direct instruction as to his will and law.

If we further assume the Divine benignity and mercy, which most writers on natural theology regard as proved independently of revelation, our argument becomes still stronger. Benignity in its very essence craves recognition and communion. Love does not conceal itself from those whom it blesses. If God be a father, his paternal attributes of necessity involve self-revelation. That he should have left his being to be inferred or surmised; that he should have given his children neither instruction, warning, assurance, nor hope; that he should have wrapt them in impenetrable and invincible ignorance, as to the greater part of what they yearn to know concerning him; that he should have suffered those of them who would gladly do his will to be bewildered and doubtful as regards that will; that he should have abandoned the less dutiful to waywardness and guilt, without a single appeal to that filial feeling which often lies deep in the very worst heart, and becomes an efficient means of repentance and reformation; this is so atrociously unfatherly, — so utterly opposed to what our own natural affection renders probable, that we must set it aside as an untenable hypothesis. The fatherhood of God and revelation, then, suppose and imply each other. If the former be a doctrine, the latter is equally a postulate, of natural religion. If God has withdrawn himself forever from direct communication with men, then, whatever else may be his relation to them, — Creator, Sovereign, Judge, — he is not their Father.

On these grounds we claim that revelation rests for its intrinsic probability on the basis of natural religion. The denial of revelation rejects the fatherhood of God, casts doubt on his benignity, negatives the inferences that flow from intelligent design, and, if it does not land us in atheism, plunges us into the hardly less dreary mist and rayless gloom of pantheism, of a self-energizing and self-organizing nature, an *animus* or *anima mundi*, which can be the object of neither trust, reverence, nor love.

Here we are met by the objection, — On these grounds revelation should have been primeval and universal. I answer, in the first place, that to no one who admits that God has ever made a revelation of himself will a primeval revelation appear improbable, to few doubtful. If we admit the authenticity of the Hebrew Scriptures, revelation was coeval with the creation of man. The religious history of mankind as recorded in the Old Testament corresponds with what on *a priori* grounds might seem natural and probable on the part of a father God ;— frequent direct interposition in the infancy of the race ; rudimentary instruction and progressive methods of discipline during its adolescence ; a full and final disclosure of truth, law, motive, sanction, recompense, for its maturity. And while I believe that Christianity may stand firmly on its own basis and be authenticated by its own evidence, I contend that, as the close and consummation of a series of revelations, it presents the more manifest tokens of its accordance with nature, with the progressive development of art, science, and civilization, with the law of growth and the sucession of epochs, which we trace everywhere in creation, read in the strata of the earth's surface, and discern even in the genesis of the solar system and the stellar universe.

Leaving Scripture aside, we have numerous vestiges of a primeval revelation. A theogony, a birth of the gods, forms a part of the mythology of all nations,— fabulous tradition thus running back to a time when the popular deities had not begun to be, and generally to a time when there was a single divinity, whose offspring were subsequently born to a rival or superior godship. This tradition has for its only possible historical interpretation a pristine state in which men worshipped one God, (how taught, except by revelation from himself?) and from which they gradually lapsed into hero, nature, or idol worship. Of parallel import is the tradition which represents a Saturnian age, a state of simplicity, justice, and innocence, a divine rule recognized and felt among men, as the earliest phasis of society, and fraud, violence, and sensuality as intruding forces through which the earth ceased to be a paradise. This, translated into history, means that the knowledge of the right and the good was in the keeping of the fathers of the race, (how but by revelation?) and was lost by their posterity.

Now, if there was a primeval revelation, the fact of its loss by the greater part of mankind is in accordance with the analogy of nature; for both the influence of character on belief, and the suffering of children and posterity from the faults, crimes, and guilt of parents and ancestors, are well known and universally recognized laws. Pure and noble beliefs cannot be retained with a corrupt heart, or transmitted by a corrupt ancestry. In all time, moral depravity has left its trail on the intellect, and each generation has inherited the errors and falsities of the preceding age. Had man's religious belief and growth obeyed other laws, then religion would have been an anomaly in human nature; and if revelation had been subject to other laws, then revelation would have been anomalous and unnatural. Is it maintained that a supremely good Creator could not but have replaced the forgotten revelation, everywhere and in each generation, by new communications from himself? In order to this, he must have abrogated the law by which children inherit mentally and morally from their parents,—a law which is of unspeakable benefit as a constant motive to healthful activity and diligence, and an effective agent in human progress and improvement. Indeed, successive generations could not be sustained as moral beings, were there a direct interposition to replace the losses of each generation, and to restore the children to privileges forfeited by the parents. In a world so constituted, there might be a splendid pageant of divine administration, but there could be no human forethought, energy or self-dependence.

But it may be asked, Why should Christianity, the perfect religion, have been withheld from the first four thousand years of human history? Be it true or false, does not its arbitrary promulgation at a precise period of time take it wholly out of the range of natural development, so that it must stand or fall on its claims as absolutely supernatural? I answer, that if there was no reason other than the sovereign, unconditioned will of the Creator for the epoch of its promulgation, — if it would have taken its place as fitly at an earlier or a later period, — then the question concerning it has no pertinency in our discussion of natural religion. But, on the other hand, if Christ came in the fulness of time, when the world was prepared for him, no sooner, no later, then was his advent as natural as are the phenomena of the successive seasons, and there is as much philosophical exactness as poetical beauty in those sacred words commonly applied to him: "He shall come down like rain upon the grass, as showers that water the earth." Let us try the question.

The leading characteristic of Christianity is, that its disclosures reach through eternity, — that its sanctions are drawn from a retribution beyond the grave. It is only civilized man that can be efficiently influenced by motives of this class. The roving savage has neither the power nor the habit of calculating and depending on the future. He knows not and cares not what will be on the morrow. He has no permanent residence, but pitches or strikes his tent as the caprice of the moment may dictate. He lays no plans, exercises no forethought, ventures no predictions, and lives entirely in the past and present. There is nothing in his mode of subsistence, which should make him dwell with either hope, doubt, or fear on the future. To impress on such minds a profound and enduring sense of a distant and limitless future, is in the nature of things impossible. Modern missionaries have found and pronounced it so, and the wisest of them admit that they must civilize heathen nations in order to make Christian institutions permanent, and that they must therefore imitate the patience of Him who, though he purposed man's redemption from the foundation of the world, waited forty centuries or more for the fulness of time to arrive.

Now this wandering, unsettled life was the natural condition of the human race in its early infancy. It was the condition of the major part of the race for many centuries. It was the condition of the Jews and of most of the Asiatics in the time of Moses. Hence the appropriateness, and therefore the naturalness, of the Mosaic revelation. A religion with temporal sanctions was precisely what the Hebrews and the age of the Exodus needed. Christianity was too far-reaching, too spiritual, for the apprehension and faith of such a horde of nomads as the exiles from Egypt, — a horde much resembling those that now range over the steppes of Tartary. I regard it as one of the most manifest tokens of the Divine origin of the Mosaic system, that it was silent with regard to a future life, and promulgated temporal rewards and punishments alone. This was as far as the forethought of the people and the age of the great lawgiver could go, and the attempt to draw motives from beyond the confines of mortality would have been useless and abortive.

But the institutions of Moses gradually changed his nation from a pastoral into an agricultural people, from a wandering into a settled community, and introduced among them the arts and refinements of civilization. Meanwhile the same process was going on in many lands, and was culminating in Southern Europe. In morals there was indeed no progress, nay, rather a retrograde movement. But civilized man always acquires the habit of looking forward to the future and providing for it, of looking far along the ages and laying plans for the benefit of even remote posterity. Civilized life cherishes forethought, and makes men live more in the future than in the past or present. This forecasting habit had its genesis and growth in the leading nations between Moses and Christ. With it had sprung up everywhere a vague belief in man's immortality; for, as soon as men thought of the future, the instinctive desire of continued existence took an objective shape, and, though without adequate proof, assumed a strong hold on the faith of large classes of enlightened men, both Jews and Gentiles. Thus, in a civilization, corrupt indeed, yet endowed with forethought, and prepared to occupy the domain in the eternal future offered to its belief and endeavor, was a matrix provided for the birth and growth of Christianity.

At this time, too, not only was civilization in the ascendant, but almost the whole civilized world had become united in the Roman Empire, so that every pulsation of intellectual and spiritual life was felt across continents, and almost from the Atlantic to the Pacific shore of the Eastern hemisphere. The union of so many and diverse nations under a single sovereignty multiplied avenues and modes of intercourse, created a community of language and of thought, and thus presented a more favorable condition of the world for the promulgation of a religion fitted to be universal, than had ever existed before, or has recurred until the present century.

Had Christ come earlier, he would, as we have seen, have found men too unsettled and improvident in their worldly habits to accept a religion whose treasures were to be laid up in heaven. Had he come later, even the area of civilization would have been contracted in the decline of the Roman Empire; while there would have been wanting the general currency of the Greek tongue, the far-reaching filaments of international union, and the homogeneous elements which, notwithstanding the vast diversity of races, pervaded the Empire in its palmy days, and favored the almost simultaneous diffusion of the new religion throughout the civilized world. But if Christianity was thus promulgated at the very time when need, preparation, and opportunity concurred to crave, foster, and diffuse it, then was its advent postulated by man's and God's nature. Its Author's birth and life, miracles and resurrection, supernatural though they be in the common acceptation of that word, are in a profounder sense pre-eminently natural; and had that age passed away unmarked by the coming of Him whose name makes it illustrious for all eternity, what would have been called the natural order and sequence of human experiences and earthly events would have been in the last degree unnatural.

If the argument of this Lecture is not fallacious, I have shown you that the antecedent probability of revelation is a doctrine of natural religion. Let it not be thought that this is a matter of mere words, and that the question of the truth or falsity of Christianity is in no wise affected by our vindicating or disclaiming for it a coincidence with natural religion. It has been the habit of Christian writers and preachers to represent the Christian revelation as something abnormal, exceptional, in antagonism to nature, an intrusion on the order of creation, and therefore not antecedently probable or intrinsically credible. It has not been unusual to admit that the facts connected with the promulgation of Christianity are in themselves improbable, and then to set over against them the still greater improbability that the array and mass of human testimony in behalf of those facts should be false. Now this weighing of opposite improbabilities is a delicate and doubtful process, and few minds hold so even a balance as to be safely intrusted with it. That which is in itself improbable, is made scarcely less so by the heaping up of remote testimony, however strong. With the temper of the present age, prone to question authority and to rely on intrinsic criteria of truth, an argument like that of Paley's Evidences is full as apt to create scepticism as to confirm belief.

No one can attach a higher value than I do to the attestations to the genuineness and authenticity of the Gospels so industriously gathered by Paley, Lardner, and the great divines of their school. To my mind, no series of events in ancient history stands on so solid a basis of human testimony as that which sustains the history of Jesus Christ, with its inseparable accompaniment of marvel and miracle. But I confess that this testimony seems to me immeasurably stronger in behalf of what is intrinsically probable and natural, than it would in behalf of facts in themselves unnatural and improbable. Testimony should never have an unnecessary strain laid upon it. It is adequate to confirm what it is inadequate to establish. Even in a court of justice, the skilled advocate deems it necessary to make the theory of his case a programme for his evidence, and is very chary of producing witnesses whose testimony diverges from that theory, even though it be substantially on his side; and circumstantial evidence which establishes an assumed theory of a case is more likely to break down opposing witnesses, than to be neutralized by them. Of the testimony for the Gospel history, the limitations of my present course will not allow me to treat. But my argument is this: The testimony — varied and strong — which may be adduced in corroboration of the genuineness and truth of the Gospels is urged in behalf of what is intrinsically natural and probable, independently of testimony. The Divine nature is virtually pledged to reveal itself. Revelation has its place in the circle of natural needs, of necessary truths. The Christian revelation, coming as it did when the world was best fitted to receive it, meets an inherent want, a universal craving of mankind, the desire of all nations, the prophecy of all antecedent ages, the earnest postulate of the religion of nature.

LECTURE III.

MIRACLES.

In my last Lecture I showed you that natural religion renders revelation probable. But revelation needs to be authenticated. Unless authenticated, it is no revelation. It is maintained, however, by many, that divine truth finds its sufficient evidence in the human consciousness, and that therefore any authority from without is superfluous, and intrinsically improbable. The following is a fair statement of a theory, which has among its advocates not a few ingenious thinkers and excellent men of our time, and which seems to be the phasis of belief entertained by the greater part of the latitudinarian members of the English Church, whose recent writings have attracted so much attention on both sides of the Atlantic. The Hebrew prophets, the Christian apostles, and Jesus Christ himself, were neither the subjects nor the workers of miracles. They were good men, Christ pre-eminently good. All men, in proportion to their moral capacity, are the recipients of teaching and inspiration from God, and these men, from the intensity of their religious genius, had a larger capacity of divine illumination than belongs even to the better portion of mankind in general. But they had no other authority than that which accrued to them from their superior capacity and excellence. They stood in no official relation to mankind, other than that which we should bear if we had similar capacity and excellence. Their teachings address themselves to our receptivity, and are truth to us only so far as they accord with whatever of divine illumination there is in us. Our inspiration is the only test and touchstone of theirs. What we do not feel to be true, we have no reason for believing to be true. What is not in our own consciousness is none the more sacred to us because it entered into their belief. They were not incapable of error in matters of religion, and we are right in rejecting as error whatever in their teachings does not harmonize with our highest conceptions of God, of duty, and of a future life.

To this theory I would reply, first, that it covers only a portion of the ground occupied by the Scriptures and religious teachings. There are, I grant, some subjects of prime importance, as to which we may verify the truth by our own consciousness, and as to which the consciousness of a sincerely good man may be regarded as infallible. This is the case with cardinal virtues and fundamental duties. The consciousness of every man who has obeyed the precepts of the Sermon on the Mount attests their coincidence with the Eternal Right. I trust that there are many of you whose belief in the Beatitudes with which that Sermon commences could not be made stro ger, were they at this moment miraculously republished in your hearing. The interior consciousness, closely interrogated, also confirms the reality of a righteous retribution, which works in the soul's experience even when it leaves no outward sign. But there are other departments of religious truth, as to which even moral perfection might fail to give certain knowledge, and in which consciousness offers no adequate test. Thus, as I showed you in a former Lecture, a good man's mere desire for continued existence, and his opinion in accordance with that desire, are no proof of immortality. There may, for aught we know, be physiological reasons why life should cease when the body dies; and if so, no height of moral excellence or of spiritual illumination could authenticate the heart-testimony to immortality which would still be borne by a soul fitted for the life eternal, and debarred from it only by physical hinderances too occult for its appreciation. In this matter we crave not the consciousness of one who feels, but assurance from one who knows; and who can know unless he has learned directly from God? To specify another subject of prime practical importance, one of the most interesting of all questions is, whether God exercises a paternal providence over us individually, or whether we live under an administration generally beneficent, but under which the individual may be a sufferer and a victim without offset or countervailing benefit. Now the best man that ever lived cannot by virtue of his goodness enter into the Divine consciousness. He may be fully persuaded of the benignity of the Creator, — he may earnestly crave all that the Christian believes about the providence of God; yet so conceivable is it as to have been the belief of many excellent men, that this minute individual providence is in the nature of things impossible. None can resolve this question except on the direct authority of the Divine mind.

Again, it is admitted that the consciousness of spiritual truth belongs only to the highly developed moral nature. One knows by consciousness only what he has experienced. The safety and blessedness of virtue have entered into the consciousness of none except the virtuous. But bad men are as much in need of religious truth as good men, and to them it must come from without, before they can have its evidence within. They must be led to virtuous acts before they can have the self-consciousness of virtuous men. And in order to secure their belief, and so to induce them to make their first experiments of moral truths which they will subsequently know by experience, there must be teaching that shall rest on recognized and infallible authority.

There is, then, need not merely of Divine illumination, but of authoritative revelation, first, to give good men the certainty of those things beyond the scope of consciousness which it concerns them to know, and, secondly, to assure bad men of those moral and spiritual facts and truths, the knowledge of which may lead to their repentance and reformation.

There are two methods in which this knowledge might be communicated. It might, in the first place, be given to every human being in some way in which he could recognize it as Divine revelation. This, however, would overbear moral agency, annul the power of choice, and make virtue and piety involuntary and inevitable, and therefore characteristics not of self-determining individual wills, but of a race of automatons, passively subjected to the Supreme Will.

The second alternative method is to commit Divine revelation to individuals chosen for that purpose, and to render it liable to those conditions of investigation, proof, and acceptance or rejection, which are attached to all other subjects on which man is left to exercise his functions as a free moral agent. This desideratum is met by a revelation resting on evidence adequate, yet not irresistible, — within the reach of inquirers, yet not forced upon them against their will, — open to scepticism, yet with ample resources for converting honest scepticism into confident belief. But in what must this evidence consist? I answer in one word, In miracle, that is, in phenomena aside from the usual course of nature, which are equivalent to the direct voice or the manifest seal of God. We can conceive of no other way in which a revelation can be promulgated as such. God without miracle might impart to the mind of an individual man so strong a persuasion of certain truths that he should absolutely know them to be true. But he has in that case no tangible, communicable evidence of these truths. To any other mind they are simply his opinions, not God's revelation. If he proclaims them, it must be on his own authority, backed by such reasoning as he can command, and if they lie beyond the sphere of consciousness, by no conclusive reasoning. But let him perform such an act as none can perform by the exercise of his own powers; let him give sight to a man born blind, or hearing to one born deaf; let him lift a dead man alive from the bier, or call forth from the sepulchre one who has lain there four days, — then, if he talks of duty, God, and heaven, if he proclaims truths beyond the realm of consciousness, his hearers know that they are virtually listening to the voice of God, that the Divine testimony attests his utterance, and that his words are absolutely and infallibly true.

It is said, indeed, and rightly, that a physical fact cannot prove a spiritual truth. But it may attest a truth-teller. It may invest him with the right to be believed. The scepticism that actually exists in the community concerns the occurrence or the possibility of miracles, not their trustworthiness as testimony. There may be among you, perhaps, some who do not believe in miracles; but were an undoubted miracle to be performed this moment in your sight, and were he who performed it to connect with it such statements with regard to unseen, spiritual, future things as you had never heard before, there is not one of you who would not believe all that he said.

The proof of the miracles recorded in the Bible, it forms no part of my plan to present. But in the residue of this Lecture I shall attempt to show you that miracles belong to the religion of nature.

Miracles are, in the first place, a demand of human nature, and an almost universal belief of mankind. They enter into the traditions of every people, and either lie at the basis, or are incorporated with the legends, of every religion. Even religious unbelief does not rid the soul of the appetency for them. We have the record of not a few cases in which avowed infidels, even atheists, have been tortured by superstitious fears, and victimized by feeble credulity as to apparitions and events aside from the common course of human experience. Every brief reign of infidelity has been succeeded by a recoil toward easy belief in marvels and wonders from the unseen world. At the present moment, the proclivity toward the dominant form of necromancy is immeasurably stronger among those who reject than among those who receive the Christian miracles. None are so ready to give heed to the drivellings and insane vaticinations of hyper-electrified women personating the voices and desecrating the memories of the honored dead, as those who deny the resurrection of Christ. The instances of the utter non-receptivity of miracles, even in this sceptical age, are less numerous than those of congenital malformation or of idiocy; while during many periods of the world's history they have been too sparse to leave either record or memorial. So far is the uniformity of nature from being a fundamental law of human belief, that appetency for the abnormal might with much greater fitness be deemed an element of man's nature, the sporadic exceptions to it seeming little else than defective specimens of their race. The multitude of confessedly false reports of miracles only strengthens my statement; for, if miracles not only have never taken place, but are opposed to the laws of belief, how is it that the entire history of belief is full of them? Counterfeits imply a genuine paradigm. The eleven false *ancilia* in the temple of Mars were forged after the pattern of the one that fell from heaven. Fiction takes its rise only from verisimilitude, and obtains currency only by its analogy to fact.

The true interpretation of the appetency for the marvellous is in this wise. Because man is spirit as well as body, and gravitates toward the unseen future while he lives in the present, there is a demand in his nature that the barrier between the material and the spiritual be at some point ruptured, the veil between the seen and the unseen somewhere parted, the realm of the dead revealed to the knowledge of the living. In no age, under no culture, has this demand been silent or inactive. It has interrogated the stars, peered into the entrails of slaughtered victims, explored the seat of life in human sacrifices, enacted the foul and horrible orgies of magic and witchcraft. And Christianity is natural religion, because it meets this demand, and satisfies this need, — because it has its authentic voices from the parted heavens, its manifest forth-reachings of the everlasting arms, its souls rendered back from the death-slumber, its immortality made manifest in the risen Jesus, — because it answers the questions which man cannot help asking, and feeds the desires which are as inseparably a part of his being as are love and memory and hope.

I would next remind you that miracles, so far from being inconsistent with the known system of nature, have confessedly constituted a large part of the history of the physical universe. By a miracle we denote an event which occurs without any proximate cause adapted to produce it. What, then, was each separate creative act of the Almighty, if not a miracle? The races of organized beings now succeed one another by established laws; but the first man, the first elephant, the first bird, the first tree, was a miracle. There was no antecedent physical cause for the shape, or size, or organization of the first-born of each family. The details might have been indefinitely varied without any failure of adaptation to surrounding objects. Man might have had as many eyes as the spider, the dove might have had four wings, the ox a trunk like the elephant's, so far as any antecedent reason was concerned. If we suppose an intelligent witness of the creation, each new substance, each organized form, each living being, must have been as literally in his eyes a miracle, an effect without a material cause, a direct act of the Omnipotent Will on lifeless matter, as to us would be the sudden reappearance alive of a man whom we knew to have been dead. And on the very grounds on which miracles are objected to as inconsistent with the laws of nature, and unworthy of the immutable Creator, an intelligent being who had existed before the earth was inhabited might in subsequent ages have refused to believe that it had any inhabitants, and have pronounced his brother-spirits who professed to have seen them impostors or dupes; for not an act of forming power or organizing wisdom can have obeyed any law but the attributes of Him to whom all things wise and good are possible. The objector to miracles can have no more appropriate or logical answer than those words in the poem of Job, which the Almighty utters out of the whirlwind: "Where wast thou when I laid the foundations of the earth? Hast thou entered into the springs of the sea? Or hast thou walked in the search of the depth? Have the gates of death been opened unto thee? Or hast thou seen the doors of the shadow of death? Knowest thou because thou wast then born? Or because the number of thy days is great?" When I contemplate the diversity of the creation, the infinity of resources which it exhibits, the miracles beyond thought which it offers to our view, dull, leaden uniformity from the creation onward seems the least probable theory. I expect to see the leading epochs in the spiritual, as they were in the material universe, marked by miracle; new life for men's souls attended and attested by visible signs of Omnipotence; the promulgation of the Divine truth and love accompanied by the shaking of the powers of nature, and the upheaving of restored animation from the realms of the dead.

But it may be alleged that, whatever may have taken place in the beginning, man has had experience only of a uniform system and inflexible laws. This, however, you will perceive, is denied by the only authority on which it can be asserted, — human testimony. We can know that miracles have not occurred only by the consenting negative testimony of all mankind, and we have seen that the vast preponderance of man's testimony is in the affirmative, — that the belief in miracles is almost universal.[1]

Let us, however, examine this question of uniformity by the light of science. That in the highest sense of the word the system is uniform, I cannot doubt; for it cannot be otherwise than consistent in all its parts with the attributes of its sole Creator and Supreme Legislator. There can be no contrasts that are not comprehended in a broader generalization, no discords that are not embraced in a more subtile harmony, no divergent tendencies which do not beyond human vision converge in ends worthy of the wisdom, declarative of the love, of Him from whom behind human vision they issued on their several tracks and missions. But in the common acceptation of the term, the system of the universe is not uniform. Astronomy reveals no unvarying type in the structure, environments, and movements of the heavenly bodies. There are in the remotest outlying provinces of telescopic vision nebulæ unresolved, and, as is believed by many astronomers, unresolvable. It matters not whether these nebulæ are in the process of consolidation, but at earlier stages of their physical history than the stars which present a sharply defined disk, or whether they are permanent conglomerations of nebulous matter. In either case, the field of telescopic vision presents as concurrently under the Divine jurisdiction two different classes of celestial bodies, which must of necessity manifest unlike phenomena, be controlled by different orders of physical laws, and bear widely different relations to

[1] Hume's celebrated argument against miracles is a mere *petitio principii*. He assumes, in defiance of multitudinous testimony to the contrary, that miracles are opposed to the experience of mankind, and maintains that therefore no testimony can substantiate them, — forgetting that the experience of mankind can be ascertained only by testimony.

their secondaries, if they are centres of systems, and to animated nature if they are, either or both, inhabited. The binary stars, revolving about their common centre of gravity, hold an anomalous place in the heavens; for the mutual relations of each pair of these celestial *gemini*, and their relations to other heavenly bodies, can be neither explained by analogies drawn from our solar system, nor embraced in our theories of the single stars. In our own system, too, there are wide diversities. The diurnal rotation of the planets — the most important of all their movements, if we consider them as inhabited worlds — divides them into two classes, the smaller and nearer planets having days more than twice as long as those of Jupiter and Saturn. The unequal distribution of satellites in the system, the solitary revolution of Mars, the gorgeous retinue of Jupiter, the marvellous environment of Saturn, are differences which science blends in no theory, legitimizes by no laws, harmonizes by no sweeping generalization, but can only point to the inscrutable will of Him who has made one star to differ from another star in glory. The comets, too, remain anomalies in the system. What uses they subserve, what dreary depths or glorious heights of space they penetrate in their aphelion, we know not, and on earth can never know. Hardly to be recognized by marks of identity when they are reputed to return, or, if cognizable, never keeping tryst with the astronomer, but before or behind his appointed time, it may be doubted whether they are better understood now than when their advent spread terror among the nations; and in them are the hidings of His power, and a stern rebuke on the arrogance which would limit the outgoings of Omnipotence, drop the line and plummet of ignorance into the fathomless abyss of the Divine counsels, and circumscribe the immeasurable creation within laws and limits of its own devising. Equally irreducible to any comprehensive hypothesis are the asteroids, — that cluster of planets so strangely multiplying under the telescope where our antecedent theories might lead us to look but for one. Has there been a miracle in that region of the heavens? We have indeed set aside the old notion of disruption from some impinging contact or explosive force, and the kindred supposition that moral causes have left the record of an outraged Deity's righteous displeasure in a shattered world. But why this pristine parting of the nebulous ring, which, for aught that we can see to the contrary, might have globed itself in undivided unity? Suffice it to say, that here is a diversity with no cause that we can trace, a lacuna in our system of the universe, a caveat against the presumption that would crowd within its own narrow hypotheses all the possibilities of nature. Whence come the meteoric stones? Of origin foreign to our planet, or at least proceeding from sources that elude our search, their motions reducible to no known law, they indicate that we are surrounded by forces which we cannot measure or calculate, that there are ordinances of the heavens which we have not yet learned to register; and they may well make us cautious in applying the limitations of our theories to events, if more significant to us, not one whit more abnormal, which may have occurred in connection with the religious history of our own planet.

I doubt not that there are intelligences that can trace and comprehend the perfect harmony of the universe, and can see the vast circumference of creation girdled by the inscription, "God is one." The point which I would urge is this, — In the system of the material universe there is seeming diversity, and even contrariety of plan, where we believe that there is only harmony and unity. We, therefore, have no reason to deny that in the administration of human affairs there may have been like seeming diversity and contrariety, as there must have been, if at certain periods and at certain places the action of proximate causes has been suspended, and Omnipotence has wrought on material forms with no intervening agency. As to anomalies in outward nature, we accept the testimony, not of our own senses, but of competent and disinterested scientific observers; — in the case of miracles we have the testimony of competent and more than disinterested eye and ear witnesses, — *more than disinterested* I say; for loss, shame, stripes, and death were the price expected and paid for their testimony.

But there still lies in many minds so profound a sense of the inviolableness of general laws, as to make them sceptical as to miracles, though sustained by the strongest evidence. We shall be prepared to discuss the inviolableness of general laws when we have proved their existence. Their existence is a mere assumption, probable, plausible, but resting on no positive ground of knowledge or necessary inference. That certain consequents which we call effects are wont to follow certain antecedents which we call causes, we indeed know, and to the extent of these regular sequences we can expect, plan, and act with confidence. But how numerous are the events which we cannot calculate, — as to which the philosopher of the nineteenth century after Christ has as little foresight as the barbarian of the nineteenth century before Christ! How know we that what we call general laws extend any further than is needed to assist our calculations? How know we that beyond this very limited range a discretionary Providence may not be the only law? Mark, — I by no means assert this, — I am not inclined to believe it; but he who objects to well-authenticated, but anomalous facts, on the ground of general laws, is bound to demonstrate those laws before he uses them in argument.

This demonstration is rendered the more difficult by the results, or rather the non-results, of inquiry into efficient physical causes. Six thousand years of research have failed to reveal in matter inherent powers that produce motion, organization, growth, transformation. We talk, indeed, of gravitation, caloric, electricity, magnetism, as if we knew what they are; yet these are but euphemisms for our ignorance, — fence-words set up at the outermost limit of our knowledge. In the impossibility of detecting, and even of imagining, an inherent force in brute matter, we are constrained to refer all power to mind, intelligence, volition; and the latest phasis of physical science, which represents force as one, and its forms as mutually convertible, is but the philosophic expression of the anthem of all pure and clear-seeing spirits in heaven and on earth, " Of Him, and through Him, and to Him are all things."

There is nothing, then, in the laws or forces of nature, which forbids our belief in the occurrence of events that seem abnormal, if there have been epochs in the Divine administration when such events could best subserve the purposes of the Creator. Nature is synonymous with God. Whatever is consistent with his attributes is natural. But it is not natural that we should know all that it was ever possible for God to do, — that his administration should be in all its parts level with our approximate philosophy of matter and of mind. Yet the entire argument of Baden Powell, the most able and reverent among the recent expositors of naturalism, is utterly baseless, if it be once admitted that the scope of Powell's mind is less than coextensive with the Supreme Intelligence. Were we to take even the popular view of miracles, as the mere arbitrary setting aside of the natural course of events, of the usual order of cause and effect, I know not why He who ordained and governs that course and order may not have suspended it at His pleasure and for His own benign purposes. His decree is the immediate cause of every death that takes place, as truly as it would be were death the exception, and continued life the rule; and if the death-bed, the bier, and the sepulchre have in some single instances rendered back their dead, this was manifestly as much within the scope of His power as it is to decree the death of those who are daily dying all the world over. If we assume that at marked historical epochs his will has, on grounds of spiritual utility, departed from its accustomed method of procedure, and set aside the wonted procession of physical antecedents and consequents, all that we need to vindicate the perfect naturalness of such miraculous events is the *dignus vindice nodus*, the occasion worthy of the Divine intervention; and such an occasion is surely found in the revelation of immortality, the authentication of the world's Redeemer, the instauration of a new era of spiritual life, when all nations lay under the shadow of death.

But can it be maintained that miracles are exceptions to natural laws? What do we mean by natural laws? *Natural* is either an absolute or a relative term. In the absolute sense, we have seen that whatever is consistent with the attributes of God is natural, and that in this sense miracles are natural. But in the phrase *natural laws*, the term is employed relatively, and refers to the generalizing capacity of him who uses it. Natural laws to any given person are such portions and modes of the Divine administration as he is capable of reducing to system. To the savage, the comet and the eclipse are beyond the range of natural phenomena. To us, the authentic facts connected with mesmerism, clairvoyance, and pseudo-spiritualism are beyond nature; that is, we cannot trace the connection between them and their proximate causes, — we cannot classify them, we cannot comprehend them in our philosophy; but the next generation will probably do all this, and then these phenomena will be natural. How know we that the works of power and love alleged to have been wrought by Christ will not, in an age of higher spiritual philosophy, assume their place in the order of nature, as precisely what should have been anticipated *a priori* in connection with a theophany, — as the very works which could not but have proceeded from the Divine attributes incarnated in a human form, — as bound to the personality of Jesus by the same constant laws of cause and effect which make our daily deeds and words proceed naturally from our limbs, muscles, active powers, and mental habitudes? If this were maintained, by parity of reason, those who by virtue of special measures of Divine inspiration or of intimate communion and sympathy with Jesus formed a peculiarly endowed class among men, may have had, as the natural and necessary results of these peculiar endowments, powers similar in kind, though inferior in degree, to those exercised by him in whom Christian faith recognizes the manifest God. Miracles then may be natural, not only absolutely, as in accordance with the Divine attributes, but also relatively, so far as the laws and the order of the universe are concerned.

Miracles are also natural, because through them, and through them alone, the Creator stands in certain relations to his creatures, in which it is natural that he should stand. Prominent among human experiences are temptations and sorrows; they belong to the essential conditions of our existence; they are evidently a part of the Creator's design; and we should expect also to find as a part of his design efficient support against temptation, adequate consolation in sorrow. If the temptation be natural, the support is equally so. If the sorrow be natural, the consolation is equally so. Now these essential offices can be supplied by nothing short of an authoritative, that is, a miraculously attested revelation.

We will consider, first, the case of temptation. I will suppose a young man, ingenuous and of good intentions, who is placed in a position of great moral danger. A friend a little older than himself gives him judicious advice and warning, which he approves with all his heart, and means to follow. But temptations increase and multiply, his own feelings become interested on the wrong side, and evil counsellors, who have the same claim to be heard with his wise and virtuous friend, do what they can to turn the balance in accordance with their sympathies and habits. And the balance is turned. The good advice is overborne and crowded out, because it was mere advice, and not endowed with any authority. But suppose that same youth under the positive injunctions of a father, in whose loving discretion he has a confidence too firm to be shaken or undermined, — the father's authority may save him where the friend's advice would be of no avail.

Now, if Jesus Christ was merely a profound thinker, an able moral teacher, worthy of respect and deference for his wisdom and goodness, yet standing in no official relation to us, and possessing no right to be believed and obeyed, his precepts are good advice, and we shall follow them till our passions or surrounding examples induce us to forsake them; but they will have no hold upon us, no clinching grasp upon our consciences, no rightful claim to our sacred heed which we cannot help recognizing. But his miracles place him in a new and entirely different relation to us. They authenticate his absolute right to be believed and obeyed. They make his precepts the word of God, the commands and prohibitions of the Omnipotent, the eternal and immutable law of His household; and thus regarded, they have a tenacious hold, a binding force, which temptation cannot relax, or evil counsel neutralize. Have not some of you experienced the power of a "Thus saith the Lord" in these fearful crises of your moral being? Has not the entire marvellous history of the Saviour at such seasons given to his words the intense emphasis of authority, which has sustained you in the right when earthly motives were all arrayed in solid phalanx against the right? And have you not then felt that it was natural that He who suffered you to encounter the full force of temptation should have given you, in this authority which you could not set aside or reason away, an adequate support and defence?

In sorrow there is a similar need. If you look upon Jesus merely as having reached higher and seen farther than any other thinker of his age, as having anticipated even the best thoughts of our own day, in fine, as a masterly religious genius, this will seem enough for you while the shadow of death is remote from your person and dwelling. It is at such times very pleasant to think and talk about the intimations of immortality in nature and in the soul, and to feel that the same organs of research and discovery which Jesus had are yours. But when your child lies dead in your house; when a friend dear as your own being is wrestling with the death-angel, and on the point of yielding up his breath; when mounds in the graveyard are all that remains to you of those from whom to part seemed like rending soul and body asunder; when the final summons sounds in your own ears, and the voice comes to you, " Put thy house in order, for thou shalt die, and not live," — then Jesus, as a philosopher of the unseen, as a suggestive thinker, as a wonderfully clear and far-seeing mortal, can give you no support or consolation. You then want his authority, — his right to be believed. You need his works of omnipotent love. You need to behold the bier stopped on its way to the grave, the sepulchre yielding up its prey, the Crucified walking in renewed life among those who saw him die. Then, and not till then, can you feel the power of those sublimest words ever uttered on the earth, which shall echo from grave to grave till the last of the dying shall have put on immortality, — " I am the resurrection, and the life: he that believeth in me, though he were dead, yet shall he live; and whosoever liveth, and believeth in me, shall never die."

My object in this Lecture has been to vindicate for miracles their place in natural religion. I have shown you that there is in the human soul a craving and an appetency for them, as seen in the almost universal tendency to believe in them; that, so far from their being opposed to natural laws, they have formed part of the undoubted history of nature, are in accordance with those Divine attributes for which nature is but another name, and in a wider generalization may be comprehended within the circuit of natural laws; and that they are adapted to the temptations and sorrows which are among the essential experiences of human nature. So far, then, are they from being attended by any antecedent improbability, that they are capable of being established by competent human testimony, and especially by so strong an array of unexceptionable witnesses as attests the Christian miracles.

LECTURE IV.

RECORDS OF REVELATION.

In my last two Lectures I have considered the grounds of natural religion on which faith in revelation and in miracles reposes. A revelation must needs have some definite form or mode, and I propose to inquire this evening in what form we should antecedently expect a Divine revelation to be communicated and transmitted, and how far the Hebrew and Christian Scriptures meet the demands and fulfil the conditions of natural religion.

A revelation, in order to be definite, must be verbal. Men think only in words. Emotions or impressions may be communicated by looks and gestures; but truth and fact shape themselves in words alone, and are transmitted only by words.

A revelation, in order to be made availing to large numbers of mankind, must be promulgated and transmitted either in speech or in writing. The recipient of a revelation might promulgate it by speech alone, and might leave it to oral tradition. But tradition, we well know, is diluted, magnified, distorted in various ways, as it passes from mouth to mouth, and from generation to generation. In the lapse of time its authenticity always lies open to question. Thus, a large part of the traditional history of our own country is already mythical, and there are varying and opposite traditions with regard to events and personages even of the last century.

A revelation committed to so unsafe a vehicle would lose its hold on enlightened faith, and would have for its adherents only those whose ignorance made them credulous.

Writing, therefore, is the form in which we should expect a Divine revelation to be embodied for permanent use. And we should expect *authoritative* scriptures. I use the word *authoritative,* not *inspired;* for the former word, and not the latter, expresses our actual need. The mode in which the writers of an alleged revelation were influenced by the Omniscient Mind — whether they were divinely moved to write specifically what they wrote, or whether, being divinely enlightened, they wrote narratives, letters, poems, as occasion prompted, and these writings became authoritative because they were the works of inspired men — is a question of not the least practical importance. But our need of a revelation implies and includes the need of scriptures that cannot mislead us. We might as well be without a revelation, as to have one on whose record we can place no confident reliance; for how know we that the very portions of the record to which we cling with the fondest yearning may not be a foreign admixture, and no part of the original revelation? If the golden sands of truth are blended with equally glittering sands that are of no value, and it is left for us to separate the precious from the worthless, the Divine from the human, we need a revelation to teach us what portion of the record contains a revelation.

I know it may be said with truth that all language is ambiguous, and especially that, in translating infallible scriptures into other than the original tongues, there must needs be more or less of vagueness and error.

But similar considerations apply equally to writings of all kinds. There is often great ambiguity in a statute drawn by a skilful hand, and passed after careful deliberation by a body of legislators. But would there not be immeasurably greater ambiguity, were the public left to unauthentic rumor, or to unauthorized letter-writers, for the transactions of the legislature? A part of a carefully prepared document is intelligible to every reader; and as for the portions that admit of being differently understood by different minds, the range of possible interpretations is limited at the outset, and is still further diminished, or wholly done away, by the comparison and discussion of conflicting views, and of circumstances and other writings adapted to throw light on the document in question. In like manner the range of mistranslation is limited at the very first, and may be constantly decreasing with growing facilities for understanding the writing translated and its original language. Unauthentic and mixed records of revelation would give rise to a vast and endless amount of error; for every man would regard that portion of the sacred writings as true which squared with his notions, flattered his prejudices, served his interests, or temporized with his frailties; and while some readers of clear mind and pure heart might detect and eliminate what was false and worthless, others would throw away the truth and retain the alloy of error alone, and there would be no common standard by which those of either class could verify their conclusions. But in authentic and authoritative scriptures there will of necessity be some portions of fundamental truth so plainly written that none can misunderstand them; the range of diverse interpretations will be limited and measurable; there will be a common standard of judgment in the original writings; and discussion will constantly tend to the elimination of error from the belief, and to growing harmony among the believers.

This statement may be amply verified by the history of opinions in Christendom. Among persons calling themselves Christians there are three classes. First, there are those who profess to receive the Scriptures as their sole and infallible rule of faith and practice. Secondly, there are those who receive as equally infallible with the Scriptures the traditions of their respective churches, the decisions of councils, and the dicta of their ecclesiastical superiors. Thirdly, there are those who regard the Scriptures as good books for the most part, but as simply Jewish literature, not infallible, not authoritative, and containing many questionable facts and erroneous opinions. Now, with all the diversities of doctrine in the first class, there are certain fundamental truths in which they all agree, such as the personality and unity of God, the divine mission, miraculous birth, sacrificial death, resurrection, ascension, and intercession of Christ, the divine influence on the soul of man, the necessity of regeneration, and the eternal happiness of good men. Moreover, it cannot be denied, that among different sections of this class there is a constantly growing harmony of opinion and feeling, — a harmony which has been cherished, more than by any other agency, by the careful study of the original Scriptures with the perpetually increasing apparatus for their interpretation. On the other hand, we find in some portions of the second class a virtual polytheism, insomuch that the worship of God is almost forsaken for that of idols, and so entire a rejection of the spiritual element in religion, that salvation is expected on the sole condition of the observance of a ritual.

Still worse, in the third class, there are those who openly deny the existence of a personal God, cast discredit on the most important parts of the Gospel history, and repudiate the belief of a conscious immortality. In fine, if you will take the two forms of belief that have the least in common, maintained by those who derive their faith from the Bible, you will find that they have immeasurably more in common, than either of them has with the Romish formalism and image-worship on the one hand, or with pantheism on the other.

We now inquire, What sort of scriptures should we expect as the records of revelation? I answer, first, that revelation would necessarily produce a literature of a peculiar kind, and would virtually create its own records. Suppose such a series of revelations as the Christian believes to have been made, — a special divine movement extending over many ages of human history, commencing with the early patriarchs, rolling on in successive waves of light along the line of lawgivers and judges, kings, priests, and prophets, and culminating in Jesus Christ. Such a movement would necessarily leave its indelible traces in the records of human thought and experience. It would be in this respect like the great movements of the physical universe. The tornado has its track, marked by uprooted trees and prostrate ranks of growing grain. The shower in the drought of midsummer takes its path, and where it passes there are greenness, bloom, and beauty, with parched and blighted herbage on either side. Thus would it be with the mighty movement of the Divine Spirit over the souls of men. Where miracles were witnessed, where superhuman forms appeared, where voices from heaven were heard, there must have been a corresponding elevation of the mind and quickening of the emotional nature. Poetry must have taken on a loftier inspiration, a purer flow, a profounder depth of meaning. Precepts must have dropped from the pen of the wise with a keener point and a weightier emphasis. Truth, not surmised or reasoned out, but beheld as through lightning-flashes that parted the clouds and scattered the darkness about the Omniscient Mind, must have been announced with a confidence and an authority that could be derived from no other source. And if a being who bore at once the form of man and the image of God dwelt prolongedly on the earth, and conversed familiarly with a circle of intimate friends, to them, so to speak, the lightning-flash must have been continuous. The clouds must have remained parted, the curtain of darkness must have been uplifted, while they were with him. They must have been literally bathed in light. Truths ordinarily unseen must have been so long and so vividly visible to them as to leave indelible images on the mental retina, so that we should have from them self-verifying representations of nature and providence, duty and destiny, in writings which would hardly need any other attestation than the keen and deep insight they displayed. Thus would revelation of necessity make and leave its own record, and subsequent generations could gather up its literary memorials, all marked by infallible tokens of the divine movement in which they had their birth.

But it may be asked, Is it conceivable that revelation should have been left to the incidental literature that would necessarily grow from it, without some more orderly and systematic record? Can we imagine a truly divine element in writings so miscellaneous and fragmentary as the Hebrew and Christian Scriptures? If God had a message or a series of messages for mankind, would he have scattered his teachings, counsels, and promises, morsel by morsel, among genealogies, narratives of wars and revolutions, stories of human folly and guilt, dreary wastes of prosaic detail? Should we not have expected from the wisdom of a self-revealing God what men have often been wise enough to write, — a body of divinity, a compend of sacred truth, methodized under appropriate titles, so that we should have in one part of the record an outline of dogmatic theology, in another an ethical code, in another an exposition of human nature and destiny, in another a digest of the religious history of the race? The Scriptures might then be studied like a school-book, and even the child might be thoroughly furnished with an accurate knowledge of divine things, to which nothing more need afterward be added. I answer, that if a council of wise and good men had been commissioned to make a Bible with a divine revelation for its basis, they would undoubtedly have made a systematic treatise such as I have described. But of what use would it have been? Dry, homiletic, full of technical phraseology, it would have had only a very limited and slow circulation, and that confined to persons of already thoughtful minds and scholarly habits. It would have had for its readers a no larger public than Cicero's Tusculan Disputations, or at most than Taylor's Holy Living and Dying, or Baxter's Saints' Rest. Bible societies would have had their issues returned upon their hands.

Scriptures thus written would also have narrowed and belittled religious truth, — would have curtailed the Infinite not only to the dimensions of a finite mind, but to proportions which that mind would outgrow; for the intellect that comprehended all the religious truth presented to it in its early years would exceed it, overlap it, look down upon it, in the pride of its strength. All positive systems are thus outgrown. They are of use in departments of knowledge with which we are only remotely concerned, or want but a slender modicum of information. They are, too, of use to really scientific men in their novitiate, but no longer. No man becomes a proficient in any science, who does not transcend system, and gather up new truth for himself in the boundless field of research. In religion there are creeds and catechisms, man-made bibles, good in their way, which profess to teach the whole of religion. But no sooner does a man place one of these between his own soul and the fragmentary, miscellaneous Bible of which it purports to be the summary, than he dwindles into a theological pygmy, has all his powers of apprehension and reflection crippled and dwarfed, and thenceforth moves, not even in a self-returning circle, but in a constantly diminishing spiral.

One chief mark of genuineness, of accordance with nature, with what we should anticipate from the Divine counsels, in the Bible that we have, is its adaptation to a lifelong study, — its expanding breadth, and growing depth, and culminating loftiness of meaning, with the enlargement of its student's own powers, — its constantly increasing hold upon the interest, so that none read it with so much freshness of experience and vividness of curiosity as those who are most familiar with it. Study these Scriptures as long and as thoroughly as we may, we never exhaust their riches, or fail to unearth new wealth of significance. And we always find more than we seek. When we dig for brass, we get gold; when for gold, rubies and diamonds blaze upon our sight. St. Paul alone might give us work for a lifetime; in his Epistles the strata of spiritual wisdom grow more and more precious, the deeper we mine them; and one might be daily conversant with them for half a century, and then leave the world with few wishes so dear to his heart as that of renewing in heaven with that glorious leader of the Church militant and triumphant the themes in which he had inspired and guided the meditations of the earthly pilgrimage.

Again, we should expect in the records of revelation a wide diversity of form, style, and method, in order to attract widely various classes of minds. As I have said, a didactic compend would have been rejected by the mass of readers. The natural method of diffusing the seedling principles of religious truth might be suggested by what annually takes place in the diffusion of the germs of vegetable life. The seeds that spring up in verdure and beauty by the wayside, on the mountain, in the forest, sown by no mortal hand, have their seed-time provided for, their propagation in new localities insured, their harvests guaranteed, by being connected with some one or more of the ever-moving forces of nature. Some are wafted to their beds on downy wings by autumnal winds. Some are borne on the fleeces of migratory animals, to vary the panorama in scenes where their kind had never before found lodgement. Some are floated on rills of melting snow, or on rain-swollen brooks and torrents, and sown in the genial soil prepared for them by the subsiding waters. Thus would it naturally be with the seeds of religious truth. In mass they would have no power of self-diffusion or self-transmission. But look at our Bible, and see how admirably it answers this condition. In this marvellous series of books the seed of the immortal harvest, whose germination is to renew the soul and transform the character, is attached to all that can attract and interest man in his neediness and sinfulness, in his yearnings and aspirations. Here it is imbedded in the winning portraiture of some venerable saint, or in the startling experiences of some God-defying sinner; there, in the wonderful vicissitudes of a nation's fortunes, rising or sinking, illustrious or disastrous, in the ratio of its loyalty or its profligacy. Again it is borne on the sweet current of holy song. Then it forms the freight of the whole touching narrative of the Saviour's life, from the hour when angels herald his birth till they watch with the apostles his ascension on high, when the everlasting gates are opened that the King of glory may come in. Then it is conveyed in the close and pungent logic of Paul, in the terse, sententious ethical discourse of James, in the tender breathings and the ecstatic visions of the loving John. There is that in the Bible which may arrest the attention and win the regard of human beings of every age, condition, and culture, — which may fix the child's delighted interest, and at the same time kindle the imagination of a Milton or a Klopstock, initiate a Newton, a Locke, a Boyle, into a profounder philosophy than that of matter or of mind, engross and crown the life-toil of a Lardner, a Paley, a Neander. Thus in every form in which men's minds and hearts can be reached do these records convey the incorruptible seed to its genial bed in the soul, attesting the divine element in them, more than by all things else, by their fitness for human nature, by their close human adaptations, relations, and sympathies.

The miscellaneousness of our Scriptures is natural, also, because we trace in them in this very particular God's wonted method of teaching, the stretching forth of the line that goes out to all the earth, the likeness of the unwritten word that reaches to the ends of the world. Not with square and compasses of man's device has God built the earth, and meted out the heavens. His creation is miscellaneous, broken at every point, — here a sheltered valley, there a profound abyss, on one side a mountain with its summit in the clouds, on the other a leaping cataract, while off in the distance the waves lift up their voice, and in the depths above the stars move each on its separate path, and shine each with a differing glory. When I look into the Bible, I behold there the same sublime diversity, — on one leaf, as it were pastures clothed with flocks, and valleys covered over with corn, where all that grows is ripe for use, and the most ignorant wayfarer cannot reach out his hand in vain; and on the next leaf, heights and depths in which are the hidings of His power, and which it may tax the loftiest faculties of successive generations to scale and fathom. I follow the Saviour into quiet home-scenes, where kind and familiar words flow as from the lips of any holy son of man, and then go up with him on the mountain where the brightness of heaven glows in his face and gleams from his raiment, and then look on the dread mystery of Gethsemane, the bloody sweat, the agony, the angel that came to strengthen him; and for this blending, alternating, mutual interpenetrating of the genially human and the ineffably Divine, I trace only the more readily the image of the God whom in part we see and know, as we do the countenance of a brother, yet about whose throne rest clouds and darkness. I mark in the Bible the Divine

Providence in the even current of human affairs unruffled by marvel as in any common history or biography, — then replenishing the widow's wasting oil-cruse, — then spreading darkness over a whole land, rending its rocks, unsealing its sepulchres; and for this combination of the unemphatic, the quiet, the grand, and the terrible, I seem to read only the more natural and lifelike record of Him who smiles upon us in the wayside flower, and then moves in storm, earthquake, and tempest, lashes the writhing waves, rides on the wings of the whirlwind, terrifies the nations. And what though in this miscellany there be much which on a superficial reading we cannot understand, — much that transcends our use, — much, too, that is beneath the standard of our age and culture? The Bible purports to be the record of the means employed for the spiritual education of men from the birth of Adam to the end of time, and for their education for an inconceivably lofty and expanded sphere of being. In this record there would naturally be some things which had their use and wrought their work long ago, having been adapted to the culture of generations whose condition and habits we know too imperfectly to perceive the divine adaptation to their needs which may have existed, — many things which may develop their full meaning only to generations of higher intelligence and truer faith than ours, — many things, also, which, pondered and inwardly digested, will reveal new and growing depths of meaning to our own hearts, — many things, it may be, which, received into our minds, yet not fully germinating here, may spring up, and blossom, and bear fruit in heaven.

If, on the grounds which I have now urged, it be granted that a revelation was likely to be committed to writing, not in a set treatise or in a strictly didactic form, but in such a diversity of methods as to meet the endless variety of human tastes and wants, we next ask, What relation would such records naturally sustain to the manners, opinions, culture, and literature of their times? Would they, in everything except the divine truth they contained, have borne marks of their human authorship, birth-land, and birth-time, of imperfect knowledge, narrow philosophical conceptions, national habits of thought, popular imagery, provincial idioms? Or would they have been conformed to some high ideal standard, so that they should transcend all other literature of their times in purity of style, accuracy of opinion, precision of historical and statistical detail, freedom from local and national characteristics, — thus belonging peculiarly to no one century or people, but bearing an equal relation to all lands and all ages? Let us test the latter alternative.

We will suppose at the outset ideally perfect scriptures, such as we might imagine to have resulted from the verbal dictation of the Divine Spirit. But is this a conceivable hypothesis? If we admit for sacred scriptures a divine authorship in the sense in which we understand human authorship, is there any style or method of which human language is susceptible which would not fall below even our least adequate conceptions of the mind of God? Or if there were, would it not transcend the comprehension as far as it would exceed the ability of ordinary mortals? In order to be understood, would it not be necessary for the Divine Author to fall below the ideally perfect, — to descend to the common arena of authorship, and simply to indite more finished history, more eloquent didactic prose, loftier poetry, than could be found in any other writings of the time, but subject to the same standards of criticism by which they are tried, liable to the same limitations from the poverty of diction, and sure, in the progress of knowledge, the development of language, and the enlargement of the scope of thought, to bear a less favorable comparison with subsequent than with contemporary literature? Now this literary competition with man, if you will suffer the phrase, is revolting to every sentiment of reverence. But this is not by any means the only argument against the theory which would exempt sacred scriptures from the liabilities and imperfections of human authorship. Let us follow it further.

The records of revelation, in order to be transmitted to coming ages, must have their hold and do their work on the men of their own time. Suppose the age when these records are reduced to writing to be a grossly material age, and one which has only somewhat coarse material imagery for the expression of spiritual truth, the scriptures constructed on this theory must reject all such imagery, and play endless changes on the few, vague, and seldom employed abstract words and phrases which the language may afford. The classical Greek might have furnished a very few such words; I am not certain that there is one in the earlier Hebrew; the Rabbinical dialect has two or three. But such as they were, they must have been employed, and ordinary readers would have been repelled or hopelessly perplexed. Then, again, in geography, astronomy, natural philosophy, therapeutics, such scriptures must recognize no prevailing error, — no, not though it were one that had wrought itself into the current belief and speech of all men. Instead of speaking of sunrise and sunset, they must expound the laws of planetary motion. Instead of using for the sky the designation of *firmament* (which denotes a solid sphere of crystal, supposed to be at the farthest a few miles above the earth's surface), they must employ phrases that imply the vastness of celestial spaces. Instead of referring to the ends of the earth, they must explain its rotundity. Instead of calling insane persons lunatics, they must enter a special disclaimer against the influence of the moon in cerebral disease. Nay, more, we, in our enlightened century, have doubtless a great deal yet to learn, errors in our philosophy to correct, wider generalizations to make; and scriptures conformed to the absolute truth of nature and science must be on a level with the scientific world many centuries hence. Now books thus written would have been in part unintelligible to the men of their own times, and, so far as they were understood, would have run so entirely counter to their received opinions on extra-religious subjects, as to awaken incredulity as to their religious contents. Scientific truth can be legitimately reached only step-wise, often with age-long preparation for a new step in advance, often with a long interval between the announcement and the popular reception of a new fact, theory, or law. Scientifically accurate scriptures would have had laid upon them the impossible task of anticipating this progress, of revolutionizing men's notions about the universe before they knew the reasons for changing them; and failing of this, they would necessarily have failed of a hospitable reception for their religious contents. We should therefore have expected that scriptures written under the guidance of a more than human wisdom, and freighted by the providence of God with truth for the illumination and redemption of mankind, would have wasted none of their power in teaching geography, astronomy, or philosophy, but would have employed on all these subjects the current speech and method of their times, would have used the popular phraseology, though founded on ignorance, and would have concentrated all their force of representation on the great themes as to which alone they were destined to be the light of the world.

Still further, sacred scriptures needed to take with their contents proofs of their genuineness from their own down to future and far distant ages. It concerns us above all things to know whether our Scriptures were written at the times when they severally purport to have been written. But where would be the evidence of this, if they were conformed to the standard of knowledge and science existing in the nineteenth century or destined to exist in the twenty-ninth, — if in their divine perfectness of finish they were swept clear of all traces of the ruder and more ignorant ages from which we believe them to have been transmitted? Foremost among the proofs of their genuineness are these very birthmarks which they indelibly bear; — in the Old Testament numerous traces of an unhistorical method of narration, of infantile conceptions as to the extent and relations of the universe, and of such scientific notions as men had before the birth of science; in the New Testament, a Hellenistic Greek which has little in common with Attic terseness and purity, bristling all over with Hebrew idioms, with not a few untranslated Syro-Chaldaic words, — in fine, a dialect which a century after the destruction of Jerusalem could not have been written by any man living. Bishop Colenso's book on the Pentateuch and Joshua needs only an altered *animus* on the writer's part to become a plea for their genuineness. The argument turns solely on certain alleged inaccuracies and inconsistencies in genealogies, numerals, and statistics, — or, the very features which characterize all early attempts at history, and which belong emphatically to Herodotus, though he was a much-travelled, all-inquiring, painstaking seeker after historical truth.[1] Had these Hebrew writers drawn up their genealogies as if they were copy-

---

[1] When this Lecture was written, only the First Part of Bishop Colenso's work had appeared. The author has not yet seen the Third Part. The argument of the Second Part rests wholly on the literal construction of the Hebrew verb יָדַע (*know*), in Exodus vi. 3: "I appeared unto Abraham, unto Isaac, and unto Jacob by the name of God Almighty, but by my name Jehovah was I not *known* to them." The name Jehovah does, nevertheless, occur in the biographies of those very patriarchs. Yet that it was not in common use until Samuel's time and afterward would appear from its being seldom used before that period in the composition of proper names, while El was often so used, and also from the fact that, in a portion of the Psalms ascribed to David, some of which bear marks of being — while others, by Colenso's usual circular method of reasoning are assumed to be — the earliest, the title Elohim prevails, while Jehovah occurs in those purporting or assumed to be the latest. Now the Pentateuch must have been written after the name Jehovah had come into current use as the national designation of the God of the Hebrews. Therefore it could not have been written by Moses, or by any person earlier than Samuel, who probably wrote a considerable portion of it.

So far as this argument is valid, it bears not against the Mosaic authorship, but against any intelligent and honest authorship or editorship of the Pentateuch. Certainly the discrepancy on which it is founded is too obvious and too utterly irreconcilable to have escaped the notice of the man or men who first made of the five books one book, or of the people generally when they began to regard the Pentateuch as consecutive history. The author of Exodus would have stultified himself by making the statement attributed to him by Colenso, seeing that he must necessarily have been conversant either with Genesis in its finished form, or with the records from which it was compiled, in which the name Jehovah is so often and familiarly employed. The obvious laws of interpretation, the genius of the Hebrew tongue, the latitude of use which we find attached to the Hebrew verb on which the question turns, and the somewhat flexible signification which the corresponding verb has in every language, authorize us to regard the passage under discussion as denoting simply that Abraham, Isaac, and Jacob did not employ Jehovah as their accustomed and formal designation of the Almighty, — an exposition which harmonizes perfectly with the notices of their history in Genesis.

ing from accurately collated family records; had they dealt with numerals as skilful arithmeticians; had their narration been precise and methodical, like the carefully compiled annals of one of our New England towns, — he would be a bold man who would claim for their books the venerable antiquity from which they purport to have come down to us. The very characteristics of these books which have given ground for ignorant cavil show most conclusively that they belong to the early infancy of written language, — to an age when historical research, the comparative criticism of documents and traditions, and artistical authorship, had not begun to be.

Yet, while as regards all subjects except religion we should expect the authentic records of revelation to be conformed to the current opinions, the ignorances, and the errors of their times and authors, we should, on the other hand, expect to see the frequent outcropping of the Divine element in strong contrast with the human surroundings, position, and culture of those same authors. On the one hand, we should look in such scriptures for characteristics which mark the age and people whence they sprang; on the other hand, for characteristics which unmistakably mark the specially Divine origin of their religious contents. Or, to vary the form of statement, we should anticipate at once such scriptures as none but their reputed authors could have written, and such scriptures as neither they nor any other men could have written except through the direct or transmitted inspiration of God. Now, in examining our sacred books, we find precisely the contrast between the biographies of the writers and the religious contents of the writings which we should expect to find in authentic records of revelation. Take the case of Moses, who, if not the compiler of the Pentateuch, must have been the virtual author of a very large portion of it. We see him the nursling of a corrupt court, the quick and reckless avenger, even to blood, of an insult offered to a brother-Hebrew, a hunted fugitive from justice, for many years an under-shepherd in a tribe of idolatrous nomads, and during his subsequent official life hasty, irascible, and querulous. Whence, then, that theology in its sublime personal monotheism standing out alone from all antiquity, — that code of social morals so rigidly just, so touchingly humane, — that Decalogue embodying more of practical ethics and religion than the rest of mankind had conceived of till Christ came, and needing from him to make it perfect only the light of his example and the sanction of his revealed immortality? David was a rude and barbarous chieftain; his throne was disgraced, his gray hairs dishonored, by the foulest licentiousness, and by deeds of atrocious violence and malignity which even the savage manners of his age cannot palliate. Whence then those strains of lyric devotion, which more than fill the purest aspirations of the most saintly among the children of men, and which awaken no sense of irrelevancy when we think of them as the vehicle of praise and prayer for the Sinless and Heaven-Born on the eve of his crucifixion? The writers of the New Testament appear in its historical portions very far from faultless, — Peter by turns the braggart and the renegade, capable of the meanest falsehood when every manly attribute cried shame upon him, — John filled with paltry jealousy, and fiercely bitter in his resentment, — Paul the truculent and unrelenting persecutor, even of helpless women. Yet in their writings what depth of spiritual insight, what ripeness of ethical wisdom, what severity of discrimination, what a pure and lofty standard of conduct and character! We cannot get rid of the divine element. Infidels are fond of dwelling on the follies and crimes of these writers. They barb the keenest shafts of Paine's scurrility. They are a constantly recurring theme in Voltaire's Philosophical Dictionary. They often reappear in the naturalistic writings of our own day. We rejoice to have them set forth in the fullest prominence; for the greater the stress laid upon them, the more utterly impossible is it to deny that the power of the Highest overshadowed these men, and that they wrote as they were moved by the spirit of God.

I pass to another point. While we should expect in the records of revelation the current style of their birth-age and birth-land, with all its limitations, imperfections, impurities, provincialisms, and that style still further affected by whatever in each individual writer was unfavorable to finished authorship, we should also expect to find frequent marks of the Divine impulse and influence in the expression no less than in the thought. All strong movements upon the mind betray themselves in peculiarly condensed and vivid forms of utterance. Now, our sacred books bear, in instances too numerous to be specified, this mark of their alleged character. They abound in passages in which a single phrase or word is charged with a richness of meaning and an intensity of force, indicating the mightiest of all influences on the consciousness of the writer. What elsewhere would fill a tedious treatise, is here globed in a sentence or a fragment of a sentence. A metaphor, an allegory, a parable, of a dozen lines, comprehends the pith and power of a volume of didactic wisdom. The story of the prodigal son contains more soul than we can find in a whole folio body of divinity. The Twenty-Third Psalm tells more of the Divine Providence than a disquisition which it would take years to write and weeks to read. There are isolated sayings of the Bible that have formed the life-long nourishment of Christians, and given them their sufficing viaticum for their last journey. I remember an instance in which a man of fine powers and large culture said on his recovery from an attack of illness which kept him for many weeks in daily expectation of death, that his life for those weeks (and it was a perfectly happy life) was but a prolonged rumination on a brief text of Scripture, into which his whole consciousness seemed to project itself, — in which his soul was clothed as in an impregnable panoply against fear, doubt, and suffering. With other good books we gladly become familiar; their brilliant sayings fix themselves in the memory; their rhythm glides softly and sweetly through the inward ear; but it is not to these that we resort in the stress of need, — it is not these that we rehearse at the death-bed or in the house of mourning. It is in the very words of prophet and psalmist, apostle and Saviour, that men fortify themselves in trial, in bereavement, under the death-shadow.

It does not accord with my purpose, nor does it fall within the limits assigned to my course, to exhibit the positive proof — to my own mind irresistible — that the Hebrew and Christian Scriptures are the authentic and trustworthy records of Divine revelation. They in fact rest on a stronger basis of evidence than we have in behalf of the genuineness of the undoubted works of the best writers of Greece and Rome; and their genuineness is impugned on grounds on which, if admitted, we should be compelled to reject all our established beliefs with regard to the literature of antiquity. My aim has been to show you, first, what sort of sacred writings the religion of nature might authorize us to expect, and, secondly, how perfectly our sacred writings fulfil the conditions which we should establish on grounds of *a priori* probability. I rejoice to have performed such an office for these writings, — not that they need my advocacy, but that they claim every expression that I can give of my grateful trust and reverence.

LECTURE V.

THE LOVE OF GOD.

In the Lectures I have already given I have shown the accordance of revelation, miracles, and authentic scriptures, with what the religion of nature might lead us to anticipate. The *contents* of a divine revelation, however, must be in great part such as could not have been anticipated on natural grounds; for it is the depth of man's native ignorance, and his destitution of adequate sources of religious knowledge, that constitute the need and create the antecedent probability of a revelation. Yet there is one important distinction to which I solicit your emphatic heed. The *discovery* and the *verification* of truth are two entirely different processes; and the faculties which are inadequate for the former process may be amply sufficient for the latter. Thus the Copernican system could not have been discovered earlier than it was discovered; for it was not the happy conjecture of the one man whose name it bears, but it marked the stage of progress which astronomical science had attained in his day: yet, had it been announced a thousand years earlier, there was science enough in India, at Alexandria, and among the Arabs, to verify it. The rules of navigation are the progressive discovery of many centuries; and not one navigator in a thousand understands the principles on which they are based; yet three months' study and a couple of voyages will enable one to verify them. The laws of projectiles have been discovered only by the profoundest processes of mathematical analysis, and are expressed in formulas which only the trained mathematician can read; every gunner in the army and navy can verify them.

In the realm of religious truth man may verify what he could not discover. Thus, though he might not attain by his own intuition or reasoning to just views of the Divine nature and administration, he may know whether the views presented harmonize with his own observation and experience. Though he might not construct for himself a perfect code of ethics, he may, by putting such precepts of duty as are given to him to the test of practice, ascertain whether obedience to them tends to his usefulness, happiness, and highest good. Though he might not without revelation feel sure of immortality, still less of any detailed characteristics of the blessed life, he may test what is revealed to him concerning the future destiny of man by its adaptation to his nature, his desires, and his aspirations. Consciousness and experience, therefore, though they could never supply the place of revelation, may furnish the strongest possible evidence of the genuineness of a revelation. In point of fact, while Christians who are both intelligent and devout find in the historical evidences of their religion ample materials for the refutation of unbelief, their faith rests more on their own consciousness than on outward testimony. Testimony assures them that their religion is true; consciousness, that it cannot but be true. Indeed, we should antecedently expect to be able to verify the truths of revelation, some of them fully, others approximately; for if He who created the soul of man and administers the government of the universe makes a revelation, its contents must of necessity be in harmony with the souls that he has created and the government that he administers. And these contents, so far as they are thus verified, are natural religion; for they are capable of being verified only because they are in accordance with the nature of the universe and of man.

I will ask you, in the remainder of this course, to verify with me some of the contents of the Christian revelation. I would speak first of the character of God, as it appears under the light of nature to the eyes which revelation has unsealed. The prominent features of the Christian idea of God — peculiar features, I would contend, for, though they have entered into the belief of modern deists, we do not find them before Christ, except in those earlier revelations which were foreshinings of Christianity — are, first, the perfect love of God, including his paternal relation to man and his all-embracing providence, and, secondly, his holiness or supreme reference to moral distinctions. The first of these, God's perfect love, will occupy our attention in the present Lecture.

We remark at the outset, that among the ends or final causes which we have been able to discover in nature, there are none which are otherwise than beneficent. There is no one contrivance for the production of evil, — no nerve that was made to ache, no sense adapted to deceive, no process whose natural working creates misery, no faculty the normal exercise of which interferes with happiness, no portion of the system or course of nature which is intrinsically and necessarily malign in its influence, no cause of annoyance or injury which man may not, in the ordinary exercise of his powers, either remove, avoid, subdue, or utilize. Now, in a universe full of the tokens of design, this state of things could not exist, were not the Creator positively benevolent. Were he malevolent, the malign purpose would be patent and palpable. Were he simply indifferent to the happiness of his creatures, that indifference would manifest itself in the choice of the most direct means to the attainment of ultimate ends, without any reference to the tendency of those means to produce happiness or misery. For instance, death must be an ultimate, and is certainly a desirable end, in a world of limited capacity, in which each species is endowed with the power of self-multiplication; and indifference to happiness on the part of the Creator could hardly have failed to manifest itself in the preference of directness and efficiency to mercy in the choice of death-producing agencies, in which, on the other hand, a careful analysis reveals the minimum of suffering consistent with the end to be attained. So is it with the entire range of natural agencies for the attainment of ultimate ends. We can trace in no one of them the will, or (if I may use a word more strictly applicable to man) the willingness to produce suffering. There is no apparatus in nature which has an immediate or necessary tendency to inflict pain or misery.

On the other hand, enjoyment or happiness is the express and undoubted end of unnumbered portions of the universe and its administration. In the senses, the affections, and the intellect, man has many endowments, and performs many functions in no wise essential to the preservation or transmission of life, or to his mental or moral culture, and which have no possible use or office other than the production of happiness. Indeed, there is not a physical, mental, or moral power whose normal exercise is not a source of positive pleasure; and this could not be the case without a supremely benevolent design on the part of the Deity. The external world, too, is full of sights, sounds, flavors, and perfumes, which can have no end other than animal and human enjoyment. Contrivances for this sole purpose crowd upon our observation as we extend it to the lower races of animals. The myriads of organized beings that float on the summer breeze, swarm in the waters, and make the forest glad, — the numberless forms of microscopic existence that fill the very chinks and crannies of creation with sentient and rejoicing life, — all demonstrate the benignity of the Supreme Being.

The progress of knowledge and of science has been fruitful, more than in anything else, in the discovery of beneficent uses, often of obviously beneficent design, in departments of nature that had been regarded as detrimental to human happiness, — in fine, in the transfer of supposed evils to the catalogue of goods. I might almost say that physical science has done nothing else than this. It has hardly made a discovery which has not been a new revelation of the Divine benevolence, worthy to be hailed with a rapturous *Te Deum*. Thus a large proportion of the most effective remedies and prophylactics at the command of the physician are drawn from the list of poisons. The gases, which unmixed are fatal to life, in their natural combinations are salutary, in their chemical offices inestimably precious. The very fire-damp which destroys the careless miner lights our cities. The electric force, in its cumulative power fearful and fatal, is the vital force of creation; and the lightning, which leaves its occasional memento in the scathed tree, the shattered dwelling, or the lifeless human form, dispels miasma, stimulates growth, and sends a quicker, healthier life-pulse on the track of the thunder-cloud. The volcano is but the safety-valve of subterranean fires, which bear an essential part in the economy of nature. Celestial phenomena once of dire portent are now recognized as staccato passages in the harmony of the spheres. All natural objects, events, and processes are in the course of verification as good in their place and beautiful in their season; and science is fast encircling the earth and spanning the heavens with the apostolic inscription, "God is Love."

In further illustration of the Divine goodness, I would solicit your attention to the natural theology of pain. In the brute creation there is, we believe, the minimum of pain consistent with the law of death and the succession of generations. Animals in a state of nature suffer little from disease, probably still less from fear. The provision by which they prey upon one another, considered in all its bearings, is beautifully beneficent. Were they left to perish by the natural decay of their physical organization, it could be only with protracted suffering, as that very decay would prevent them from seeking the wonted means of subsistence. But the condition, whether of age or of accidental disablement, which prevents their supplying their own needs, renders them with merciful promptness a prey to their natural enemies. Moreover, so far as we know, except where domestication and full feeding make an animal indifferent to the uses of his victim, death by beasts of prey is almost instantaneous, and the life which up to that moment had known neither care, apprehension, nor suffering, goes to reinforce another equally painless life.

But man is liable to intense and prolonged suffering,

and we can fully vindicate the Divine love in man's condition upon the earth only by recognizing the moral benefit which results from the various forms of painful endurance. This, however, hardly needs a labored demonstration; for none are so ready to admit the benignant efficacy of suffering as those who have been themselves the greatest sufferers, and among those who bear all the marks of the highest spiritual culture, and at the same time of the fullest measure of conscious happiness, there are multitudes to whom we can point, not in pity, but in admiration, and anticipate the announcement which the Apostle heard in his vision of heaven, "These are they that have come out of great tribulation."

Considered with reference to its moral and spiritual ends, pain has its merciful limitations. Up to a certain point it may be borne with cheerful submission and with conscious benefit to the moral nature. When it transcends this point, one of three things takes place. Either death ensues; or some paralytic or gangrenous affection intervenes, which separates the suffering organ or member from the rest of the body, and forbids the nerves to transmit their report to the brain and the consciousness; or, if neither of these, delirium makes the soul imperfectly conscious of what the body endures, or even wraps it in a wild elysium. I hardly need remind you in what an overwhelming majority of instances either of these alternatives may be anticipated and prevented by anodynes and anæsthetic agents.

There is also a limit of age. The intenser forms of physical suffering belong for the most part to the period of active moral discipline, when pain may yield its full revenue of spiritual benefit. The sufferings of infant children are doubtless much less severe than they seem.

The infant brain is but imperfectly developed in its susceptibility of impression, no less than in its active power; in many forms of disease it is so far affected directly or by sympathy as to diminish greatly the amount of conscious pain that would otherwise be experienced; and we all know how the capacity of enjoyment, and even of absolute mirthfulness, will betray itself in children amidst paroxysms that threaten instant dissolution, and when already under the shadow of death. Thus the morbid liabilities of very young children serve the purpose of sustaining parental vigilance and multiplying those tender offices by which the ties of blood and birth are made doubly strong and dear, while comparatively little is abstracted from the joyousness of the irresponsible years of opening life. In old age we may mark a similar limitation. There is a period of decline, when, though the character still grows from its own resources, active moral discipline ceases, and the aged person seems to be merely awaiting the summons to a sphere of duty in which the worn-out body will be no longer needed. This period is seldom liable to acute disease or intense suffering. The nerves and the brain have lost much of their sensitiveness. There is often languor or weariness, but seldom continuous or severe bodily anguish. The gentle steps by which one is led through declining years are almost always the subject of grateful observation, except where vice has thwarted the kindly purpose of nature, and planted thorns of its own in the pillow of the hoary head.

Apart from its moral uses, pain serves important physical purposes. It is the sentinel against bodily injury. It is the guardian of temperance, purity, and hygienic regimen. It is the prime executive as to those natural laws which we are bound to obey, and which ought not to be violated with impunity. And in this office of pain, also, we may trace limitations that indicate the Divine goodness. Thus the pain of hunger recurs in its mildest form just often enough to induce the regular supply of our wants that is essential to health and vigor. It reaches its acme of agony at the very point at which the supply can no longer be delayed without serious injury and peril. If the supply be of necessity postponed, the pain, having served its purpose of warning, dies away, and lethargy ensues. The same is true of suffering from extreme cold. Intense pain warns the exposed person to seek shelter, with a call loud enough and long enough in most cases to effect its object without detriment to life or limb. But when the injury has taken place, when the limb is frozen, the sentinel, no longer needed, quits his post, unconsciousness of suffering ensues, and even sensations of ease and comfort may precede the fatal issue of the exposure. To the same category belongs the well-known fact, that the nerves susceptible of the most painful sensations lie in precisely those parts of the body which we can protect or heal, and which would be perpetually exposed to maiming or injury, did not their liability to pain make us careful of their safe-keeping and well-being. The seat of the severest suffering is in almost all cases near the surface. The first touch of the surgeon's knife inflicts much greater pain than the deep incision, the laceration of the flesh than the division of the bone, the wounding or fracture of the arm or leg than the lesion of those vital organs which are subject to more occult laws, and can with less certainty be guarded from injury or restored from disease. In fine, pain, with few and sporadic exceptions, is most intense where the means of prevention or recovery are generally known or easily attainable.

Now suppose a painless world. Imagine our children growing up without liability to suffering or its semblance, and our friends, our parents, those bowed with years, those who claim our devoted offices of love and reverence, subject to the death-producing agencies which must none the less exist and work, yet unwarned by admonitory sensations of pain. This state of things could hardly fail to induce neglect. The most intimate offices of parental and filial love would be superseded, and in the same proportion the affections would be deadened and their joy obliterated. Our homes would lose their endearments, their sympathies, their most grateful remembrances. There would be coldness where there is now the tenderest love, and severed existence where there is now the closest union. Imagine, too, the active portion of mankind no longer liable to suffering. What reckless exposures would there be, what unconscious neglect of physical laws, what suicidal feats of strength and endurance! The maimed would outnumber the uninjured, and the needless, foolhardy deaths would be more than those that now occur by disease and casualty combined. These considerations certainly deprive human suffering of its mystery, and bring forth rich testimony from the severest experiences of our earthly condition to the goodness of the Creator.

I have spoken thus far of physical suffering only. In verifying the Christian view of the Divine character, we encounter not only the pain that befalls men in the ordinary course of nature, but also moral evil, and the misery that flows from it. Here we must remember at the outset, that in the nature of things wrong-doing cannot be harmless. Right and wrong are not arbitrary, but essential characteristics. The wrong is in its very essence unfit to be done, and, if the right has beneficent results, it is impossible that its opposite should not have opposite results. Omnipotence can no more deprive the wrong of its power of harming, than it can make two and two five.

In the next place, free agents must needs have the power of doing wrong, in order that they may have the power of doing right; and if they have the power of doing wrong, it is impossible that they should not exercise it, at least in the earlier stages of their history, and until the entire range of moral experiments has been exhausted. The only question then is, whether this perilous gift of free-agency is consistent with the Divine benevolence. In answering this, we must suppose that the plan of the Creator would embrace every kind and degree of happiness of which finite beings are susceptible. Now does not our consciousness assure us that free-agency rightly exercised is the source of immeasurably higher happiness than can flow from all other sources combined? With what shall we compare it? With intelligence? Intelligence brings labor, care, and pain, and of itself bestows no counterbalancing joy. What we call the pleasures of knowledge or of the intellect derive their zest from the moral nature. Emotions and affections that have their source in a loyal and obedient will alone enable us to assimilate the materials of knowledge, and to make them conducive to our nutriment and growth, our elasticity and gladness of spirit. Without this moral solvent, the acquisitions of the intellect are but burdensome and oppressive crudities, ministering to our isolation, misanthropy, and restlessness. But if such be the case, it was the part of Divine love to provide for the highest form of happiness, that flowing from moral goodness, even though it were foreseen that countless multitudes would spurn the noble gift. And if moral excellence be the supreme good, then is there no more merciful portion of the Divine administration than the wretchedness that results from human guilt. The issue of sin in misery is the surest way of awakening repentance and producing reformation. Sin never looks so appalling and offensive as when it is mirrored back from its consequences to the sinner's own consciousness. By the desolation and misery into which men plunge themselves and others, they are made to abhor themselves, and to cherish purer affections and better purposes; while by the same exhibition the innocent are kept innocent, the tempted held back from evil, the virtuous confirmed in their good principles and habits, and the philanthropic urged to more vigorous efforts for the restoration of the fallen and the well-being of their race.

I have thus far spoken of the goodness of God as manifested in the general administration of the universe. Christianity goes further than this, and affirms his providence in all events, his paternal providence over every member of his human family. The Divine Providence has for its rational grounds the native inertness of matter, and the necessary omnipresence of the Deity.

Inertness — that is, the tendency to remain in its present state, whatever that be — enters into our conception of matter. As I said in a former Lecture, philosophy has abandoned the search after efficient material forces. Mind, will, is recognized as the ultimate cause of all motions, changes, phenomena, events. The laws of nature (so called) resolve themselves into wonted methods of the Divine administration. If we deny this, our only alternative hypothesis is the pantheistic conception of an inherent force, an immanent and active will, a self determining power, in matter. But when we provisionally adopt this hypothesis, we find it impossible to conceive of the initial impulse, of the beginning to be, of the self-existence or self-creation of matter; and we are thus thrown back upon the belief in a creative will distinct from the material universe, which will, as it was the sole cause of the beginning to be, must equally be the sole cause of the ever-varying phenomena of continued being, of the ceaseless change of material objects, inert in themselves, which could no more alter their mode of being than they could begin to be without a Supreme Will.

Again, the omnipresence of God is involved in the very idea of his existence. But can his be an inert presence? Where he is in the plenitude of his almightiness, can aught take place otherwise than by his will?

There is no room for the old distinction between a general and a particular providence. The former cannot be without the latter. We can make no discrimination between the greater and the less, which does not betray the shallowness of our speculations, and convict us of the folly of meting the universe with our own paltry measuring-tape, and sounding infinity with our own brief line. Do we say that God governs vast events, and exercises no direct supervision over the smaller concerns and interests of his children? What affairs even of nations, worlds, systems, are vast to him whose stars crowd by myriads the field of telescopic vision, and pave the highway of the heavens as countless as the sands on the sea-shore? And, on the other hand, what concerns of sentient, reasoning man are not vast, compared with the structure and functions of those curiously and wonderfully formed beings, bearing every token of the Divine handwork, to which a drop of water or a fig-seed is as a universe? Embosomed as we are between twin infinities, between the immeasurably immense and the inconceivably minute, we dare not set metes and bounds to the universal Providence.

> "To him no high, no low, no great, no small,
> He fills, He bounds, connects, and equals all."

A paternal providence is claimed by many as a truth of experience. The privileged and happy, if at the same time devout, see more than a beneficent order of nature and flow of events in their own conditions and lives, and think that they can recognize the Divine care and love for themselves individually. The favorite utterance of piety is, "How precious also are thy thoughts unto *me!* How great is the sum of them! If I should count them, they are more in number than the sand." There are in every happy life numerous instances in which the course of events might seem to have received a special direction for the benefit of the individual. Large portions of our lives — crises, it may be, on which our whole earthly destiny depended — have been shaped without any planning or foresight by ourselves or others, — by what the world terms chance, — by circumstances in themselves trivial, — by our coming, as it seemed fortuitously, into relation with certain persons or objects rather than with others, or at one moment rather than at another. An interview called casual, a delay or hinderance regarded as accidental, an act so slight and so utterly indifferent in any aspect visible at the time of action that there seemed a hundred chances against one that it would not be performed, has often determined all the essential events of a lifetime. A conjuncture of circumstances in itself trivial, and which a day or two, perhaps a few minutes, earlier or later would have had no traceable consequences, is often the critical moment of one's fortune, the first of a series of causes from which his whole subsequent happiness flows. It is contended that in these cases, in the absence or feebleness of proximate causes, there is a distinct revelation of the paternal providence of God.

But in dwelling on the happy experiences thus traced to the love of our Father, we must not forget that the statement we have made applies equally to adverse crises, prolonged series of misfortunes, ruined hopes, thwarted plans. The slight initial causes in whose train flow the most momentous consequences, for evil no less than for good, to men, communities, and nations, form one of the most curious chapters in human history. A striking instance occurs to me. In the Twelfth Congress, which declared the war of 1812 between this country and Great Britain, a new Senator of the United States, who voted for the war and voted with the war-party on all preliminary questions, was chosen by a legislative majority of one. A member in the majority of the legislature that elected him was chosen by a majority of one. That majority was given him by a man who had never before voted with the party that favored the war, but was induced to do so in this instance simply because the cattle of the opposing candidate had trespassed on his corn-field. Had the opposing candidate for the National Senate been chosen, the war would probably not have taken place.[1] That trespass, then, may be said to have caused the war. Now while I have the profoundest faith in a benignant providence always and everywhere, — a providence that often reveals itself in the feebleness or the fortuitous aspect of proximate causes, — I cannot but regard it as a providence that ordains not only the blessings which we desire and rejoice in, but the sorrows that may nourish our higher natures, and the retributive visitations which men or nations may both merit and need.

But while God wounds only in love, and punishes that he may restore, our language bears one testimony of very great and incontrovertible force to the preponderance of the joy-giving element in the Divine Providence. It is implied and employed in the use of the word *happiness*, — at once an atrociously irreligious and a profoundly religious word. It means that which *happens* or chances, thus excluding in its form the agency of an overruling Providence. Yet in the application of this ungodly word to felicitous events alone, we bear tacit testimony to a benignant order in human affairs; — we confess that, if we are the subjects of chance, it is of a chance that plays with loaded dice; that is, we deny the sovereignty of chance in the very act of admitting it, and affirm that of Providence in the very act of denying it; for, were events fortuitous, the *happenings* to us would be as often afflictive as they were glad, and *happiness* would never have been chosen to designate joy. While it might not be safe to reason from individual experiences, the vast

---

[1] The final vote in the Senate for the declaration of war was 19 against 13; but had the anti-war party commanded only one additional vote, the declaration would have been postponed, and in a very few days the news of the repeal of the Orders in Council would have rendered the war impossible, by removing its principal grounds and pretexts.

preponderance of pleasurable sensations over the contrary, — the system under which happiness is the rule, misery the exception, — is a clear and full demonstration of a fatherly providence, which wills and promotes the enjoyment and well-being of its subjects.

There is also an inward experience which cannot mislead us, — a spiritual providence by which we are prepared for such events as God may send, strengthened for our burdens, sustained under our trials, by resources of which we were unconscious till the stress of need, and in which we rejoice to trace the direct action of a Father, who loves us more than we can love ourselves, upon our minds and hearts. These experiences are often clear and emphatic; they multiply upon our recognition in proportion to the constancy and thoroughness of our introspection; and they leave in the most reflective and devout spirits an assurance too profound for doubt, that God is with us in his fatherly providence where we most need his inspiration and support, in the region of our sensibilities and affections.

I have spoken of the argument from experience. There is in the aggregate of human experience a counter-argument which we are bound to meet fully and fairly. I refer to the case of the multitudes, the myriads of the utterly unprivileged, — of those who have their full share of calamity and sorrow without access to the faith which might enable them to sustain their trials patiently and hopefully, and to transmute them into nourishment for the moral nature. It cannot be denied that, for unnumbered millions, if this life were their only being, or if they were destined to suffer hereafter for lack of what they had no means of doing or becoming here, it had been better that they had not been born.

But if the earthly life be for them a brief embryo-state from which they emerge into a realm of light, privilege, and joy, it is easy to conceive that their present condition subserves essential purposes of the Divine Providence, which we may not now fully understand. Let me borrow an illustration from the physical history of our planet. There were, long before man or the higher animals had birth, geological ages during which rank, luxuriant vegetation overspread large portions of the world. Forests rose in beautiful verdure, ferns and grasses clothed the plains, though there were none to enjoy the shade or to feed upon the harvest; and generations of these forests, unnumbered growths of this profuse vegetation, were swept by volcanic fires, and piled heap upon heap in massive strata. Had one of the elder sons of God, not endowed with foresight, beheld this process, he might have questioned the Divine wisdom, and asked, "To what purpose is this waste of what might feed and shelter living, reasoning, enjoying races?" But these layers of charred forests are what now sustain our fires, and feed our forges, and propel our ships, and promise supplies for human art and comfort for myriads of years to come; and all generations will bless the Omniscient Wisdom whose seeming waste is their unexhausted wealth and strength. Spiritual geology, too, may have its ages whose meaning is to be studied only in the remote future. This seeming loss and waste of souls on earth, redeemed no doubt in heaven, may have its end in the sure development and ultimate supremacy of goodness through the whole universe of God. It may be essential to the education of our race, that the history of every form of evil should be written out in gigantic characters; and the vicious experience of earlier ages may have its ultimate result in ages that shall roll on in undimmed holiness and blessedness. He who lays the beams of his chambers in the waters, while their topstone is above the heavens, may be laying the sunken foundations of that kingdom of universal righteousness, in which not future generations alone, but those too whose earthly destiny was beneath the floods of ignorance and depravity, shall have their eternal dwelling-place.

I grant that, if this life be regarded as a period of probation and the only period for all men, as it is a probationary state and may be the only one for the fully privileged, the condition of the unprivileged would be irreconcilable with the Divine love. But, so far as these last are concerned, is it not reasonable to suppose this world simply a birthplace and conservatory of spirits that are to be trained and nurtured elsewhere? Go into a plantation of fruit-trees in which orchard and nursery are combined. You will there find some trees that have soil-room and sky-room enough to reach a normal growth, and to perform their function as fruit-bearers, that is, to fulfil their destiny; and those trees are in a probationary state. Their worth will be tested by the quality and quantity of their fruit. If their fruit be poor or scanty, after suitable efforts to improve it, they will be cut down, and others will take their places. If their fruit be rich and abundant, they will be cherished with the utmost diligence. But a large part of these trees are to have their probation elsewhere, it may be in richer soil and under more skilful culture. The only aim now is to make them live, to give them shape as existences of their own order, to establish their relations with soil and sky; and when they are fairly made alive and capable of prolonged existence, they will be transplanted to the respective sites where their fruit-bearing capacity can be developed and tested.

Now the thronging ranks of the unprivileged can be compared only to these closely crowded trees planted on purpose to be transplanted. They do not get their moral training here. They do not fairly make their election between good and evil. They know so little of moral distinctions, that the wrong which they seem to choose is in no sense the choice of the soul, and may not unfitly be regarded as a mere habitude of the body. What they do get here is life, — the capacity of an endless life. They come into those relations with time and space which are essential to the detached, personal existence of a finite spirit. They are placed, also, in certain determinate relations with fellow-spirits, which may through all eternity render their social condition immeasurably happier than it could have been had they been isolated existences, each brought into being by a separate act of omnipotence. They are made each to have some experience of the straitnesses, infirmities, and sufferings of this mortal state, and none can say how essential a part this experience may bear, as a source of gratitude when God shall have "enlarged their borders," as a term of comparison by which they may know how highly they are blessed, as a starting-point to which they may measure back the path on which the Divine love shall lead them.

At the same time, under precisely this system, while to many individuals existence and the capacity of being advantageously transplanted are God's chief and best gifts, a process of education for the race is developing itself along the ages, — a process by which undoubtedly the maximum of active goodness, the most vigorous and salutary exercise of moral freedom, may be insured. Had equal privilege been at the outset ordained for all, and preserved by the interposition of Providence from age to age, human society would present only a dead level of tame and passive goodness, with hardly vitality enough to merit the noble, manly designation of virtue. There would be no room for the loftier and more heroic forms of excellence. The greatest names on the annals of moral attainment and achievement would never have been written. Nay, there would have been no place for the "name which is above every name," and for the tender reverence, profound gratitude, and warm affection which, clustering around it and rising from it with enhanced fervor to Him who so loved the world that he sent his Son, form the richest portion of man's spiritual experience. And when the world shall have been all reclaimed, when the nursery shall all be fruitful orchard-ground, there will have been created in the veins of humanity, to be transmitted to sinless generations, and to be translated to its ultimate higher sphere of being, a vastly nobler, hardier, more energetic type of moral and spiritual character than could have come into existence, had the plan of Providence been that of equal privilege for all and always.

I have thus shown you that the seeming exceptions to a benign Providence are not really objections, when viewed in connection with the intensely strong positive arguments that may be urged in its behalf.

This subject furnishes an impressive illustration of the office of revelation as regards the truths of natural religion. In the observed course of human experience there are contrasted facts that seem at first sight as utterly irreconcilable as if they flowed from the rival working of a benevolent and a malevolent Deity. There is, on the one hand, mercy, blessing, privilege; on the other, the seeming absence of all these. Nature, unenlightened by revelation, refuses to embrace these facts in one comprehensive generalization. Their harmony eludes her search. Revelation utters the word PROVIDENCE, around which they all crystallize, and opens the immortal life which proffers scope for their development in a coherent system initiated and crowned by the infinite love of God. The truth, *Providence*, belongs to natural religion; revelation furnishes the clew which leads us through its labyrinth, lets down from heaven the hand that unseals its mysteries, utters the voice that interprets its harmonies of love and praise.

LECTURE VI.

THE PROVIDENCE OF GOD IN HUMAN ART.

My last Lecture was on the Divine Goodness, and especially on the Providence of God considered as a doctrine of human experience, that is, of natural religion, and on the objections urged against it on the ground of the unequal distribution of privileges in this world. The Scriptures affirm the providence of God in a more general sense, his providence — forethought, determined provision — in the powers and faculties of man as adapted to this world and his place in it; and it is to a single branch of this wide theme that I ask your attention in the present Lecture.

Man is proud of art and skill more than of all things else. Virtue and piety are, indeed, greater and nobler, but they make men humble, not proud; and even they are indebted to the arts of civilized life for the basis of intelligence, knowledge, culture, and refinement, on which alone they can be built up in their full strength and beauty, and by means of which alone they can have their due manifestation and influence. But what man has done for himself and for his earthly home, — the wastes he has reclaimed; the cities he has built; the grandeur and beauty he has embodied in architecture, enshrined in marble, portrayed on canvas; the enslaving to his uses of the giant and wayward forces of nature; the overcoming of obstacles that once seemed insurmountable; the sovereign command which he exercises in the entire realm of material forces and agencies, — these are the burden of his unceasing self-praise; and especially we are never weary of admiring the vast mechanical and artistical progress of the last and the present generation. Meanwhile, the perpetual voice of the Bible is: "All power belongeth unto God." I have taken for my subject this evening the Natural Theology of Art, and my aim will be to show that human art is but a manifestation of the Divine Providence; that God is, as the Scriptures represent him, the sole contriver, artificer, builder, — the author of all the vast, graceful, curious, and complicated forms that grow under the hands of man; and that the achievements of our race are equally with the sun in his glory, and the stars on their circuits, and the changing seasons, "but the varied God."

Let me first remind you that in art man does nothing except what God either does or provides for in nature. He only follows out indications that are a divine directory for his procedure. He creates nothing; he only finds and uses what God has made. He does not confer properties; he only discovers and applies them. We talk of raw material; but there is none. If there were, it would forever remain so. What we call by that name has in it all that is ever made out of it. Our paving and building stones lie, in the quarry, in parallel strata, and with crystals so grouped and separated as to invite the very cleavage they receive; and the blocks in which they are laid or heaved correspond in their surfaces with the natural divisions of the mother rock. The veins and fibres of our forest-trees guide, rather than yield to, the axe, the lathe, and the plane; and they might have been of essentially the same substance, and yet so gnarled and knotted as to defy the accumulated science of centuries. Our silk we could not wind or use, had it not been first reeled on the cocoon with a delicacy far surpassing our finest handwork. We make no dyes, but dip our raiment in brilliant and enduring hues, beautiful as the rainbow or the sunset clouds, which God has treasured for us in barks and roots and insects. The telegraph is no work of ours, nor yet an invention of our time. The agent which it employs has been from creation's dawn the medium of all communication between mind and matter, brain and muscle, brain and brain; and in the phenomena of mesmerism and pseudo-spiritualism there can be no doubt that along air-lines and for indefinite distances thoughts and words are sent with the same unerring accuracy that marks their transmission on the artificial lightning-path. We have only arrested for a specific purpose a force which throbs from zone to zone, leaps from sky to earth, darts from earth to ocean, courses in the sap of the growing tree, runs along the nervous tissue of the living man, and can be commanded for the speaking wires simply because it is and works everywhere.

Permit me to carry out this view somewhat in detail with reference to water, the most essential of all mechanical agents, with which art does literally nothing of which God has not given the model or the hint.

How numerous beyond all computation are the artistical contrivances of which water is the means or the object! Not only is it the destined home of the ship, — that noblest masterwork of human genius, that most expressive type of man as the conqueror and lord of nature, — but without water how utterly impossible would it be to bring together materials for the ship, or for any other costly and complex structure! Without its diffusion in quantities and qualities adequate not only to sustain life, but to supply the thousand-fold greater demands of art, where were the triumphs of that monarch of our century, the steam-king? Now mark how perfect, as regards human industry, is the Divine distribution of water, — gathered into oceans for the world's highway, — indenting the shore in bays and creeks without whose shelter navigation would be impossible, and the ship a mere splendid conception, — radiating in rivers which alone could develop the resources and furnish the materials that freight our commerce, — branching into streams and rivulets to irrigate the meadows, to twine among the valleys, and to laugh by the poor man's door, — now falling over precipices, and acquiring force to propel the wheels of those mighty Babels that weave the wealth of nations, — now swollen by vernal thaws and rains, and bearing forests from their birthplace to the builder's axe.

Mark next the beautiful simplicity of the Divine mechanism by which the distribution is made. There is unceasing waste, and yet unceasing fulness; — the ocean replenishing the fountain, the fountain speeding with trembling haste to bear its tribute to the ocean; the river pouring its current into the great sea, and anon those selfsame waters, through cloud, torrent, brook, and streamlet, seeking the river again. The circulation of the waters is like that of the blood in the human body; — the ocean, the vast heart; the rivers, the veins that carry home its tide; the clouds, the arteries that distribute it anew; the brooks and fountains corresponding to the capillary vessels that bear the rose-tint to the cheek of youth and beauty. The system, too, is self-adjusting, full of mutual checks and offsets, the very circumstances that create the need expediting the supply. The solar heat, as it parches the continent, distils and evaporates the adjacent water of the ocean or lake, forming clouds which, like aerial burden-ships, float away with their freight of bloom and harvest wealth, and are drawn by the partial vacuum to the very regions where intense heat has most rarefied the lower strata of the atmosphere, at the same time threatening the hope of the husbandman and exhausting the fountains of man's industrial energy.

But for the numberless demands which man, more as an artisan than as a consumer, makes on nature's reservoirs, distribution is needed in immeasurably larger quantities than could be endured in the form of rain in our fields and about our dwellings, unless we were amphibious, and our grain and grasses aquatic plants. Mark next, then, the Divine providence by which the mountains that must forever remain uninhabitable are made the ocean's procreant cradle. The levity of the clouds as compared with the lower strata of the atmosphere, lifts a large proportion of them to a height at which they are drifted against the tops of the loftiest mountains, where, amid

"Unceasing thunder and eternal foam,"

or in hail and snow, they discharge their burdens, and form those fierce and rapid torrents which, as they approach human dwellings, grow deep and broad, tame and tractable, so that the very stream which had rolled huge crags and uprooted primeval forests from the mountain-side can be resisted by the feeble stroke of a child's oar, or made the servant of all work in a machine-shop.

Mark now the relation of human art to this vast system of circulation. The raft, in which form alone could lumber be delivered at its appropriate depots without labor and cost that would make a well-built house a luxury attainable by none but the very rich, simply avails itself of the ocean's feeding season and of its channels of supply, — commits itself to their swollen bosom, — forces itself upon them as the companion of their inevitable journey. The ship, hardly less essential to material civilization than is the Bible to spiritual culture, is the most passive of all creatures, depends for its motion on the sails which diminish its power of resistance and render it even more hopelessly passive, and yields itself to the very atmospheric currents which sustain the circulation of the waters by driving the clouds landward. The water-wheel, which multiplies and cheapens to an inconceivable degree the comforts and luxuries of civilized life, merely plants itself in the descending path of the stream or river, and revolves because its axis is so secured that it cannot be floated down. The aqueduct, which gushes as a fountain of health in the great city, bears the same relation to the course of the stream which feeds it, that is borne by the air-line turnpike to the serpentine road that leads by every farm-house; and depends for its flow on the gradual declivity by which the ocean-born clouds descend from their mountain-exile to their native home. Lastly, the steam-engine, the most versatile of all the works of man, — now bearing on its fire-wings migrating multitudes and costly merchandise across the waste of waters, now twisting a gossamer thread or mending a web, — is but the intensifying (though in miniature) and harnessing to the industrial yoke of the very process by which the vapor exhaled from the ocean waters the hills and makes the desert glad.

I might still further illustrate the providential element in human art by reminding you of the limitations of art. Take for an instance the cotton manufacture. The Sea-Island cotton, you know, is greatly superior to the Upland in length and fineness of staple. Now no mode of culture, no maritime dressing, no copiousness of irrigation, can overcome this difference. A profounder chemistry than ours entails on these respective soils their own peculiar growth. Nor can machinery, however delicate, compensate for this difference, so as to fabricate fine lawns and muslins from Upland cotton unmixed. Indeed, that we are able to spin cotton at all is in no sense owing to the perfectness of our machinery. There are many downy substances in nature which, to the superficial or the naked eye, offer as fair a promise of utility as cotton, yet which can never be made into thread or cloth. The late Rev. Dr. Cutler, of Hamilton in this State, memorable as a pioneer in the settlement of Ohio, was the first American botanist of his day, and was eminently utilitarian in his scientific pursuits. He cast his eye upon the common silk-weed, or milk-weed, *Asclepias cornuti*, whose seeds ripen in a most luscious bed of down, as a plant which might rival or supersede cotton, and enable us at the North to raise our own clothing, and that on soil available for hardly any other purpose. His researches in this matter gained merited attention, and, it was said, — I know not whether the story be authentic, — were the specific ground on which certain literary honors, which he on every account richly deserved, were bestowed by one of our New England colleges. But they had no more valuable result. On trial it was found that the silk-weed has an incorrigibly short fibre, and of course the spindle cannot make it longer; that it has a straight fibre, which cannot be pulled without breaking, while cotton has a curled and crooked fibre which the strong pulling of the machinery only straightens; and that it has no hooks or teeth, so that it cannot be permanently twisted, whereas the fibres of cotton are indented with teeth like those of a saw, which hook into one another when the fibres are twisted, and without which no force on earth could so twist them that they should remain twisted.

The sugar manufacture offers us a similar illustration. Sugar, in order to become fit for the market or the table, must be granulated, or formed into minute polyhedral crystals, each capable of adhering to its neighbor crystals, as in lumps, without their running together as in a paste. The sugar-cane, the beet, and the maple are the only plants of common and easy cultivation from which sugar has been successfully made. Yet, as a chemical ingredient, sugar enters into numerous vegetable productions, and into none, perhaps, more largely than into our common maize, from which the manufacture, as has been estimated, would at least double the agricultural revenue of the Free States of our Union. With this view the corn-stalk has been subjected to faithful and elaborate experiment. The juice has been expressed, and has presented hopefully all the characteristics of the cane-juice; but the modes of crystallizing the cane-juice, and all other modes that science or skill could suggest, have failed, simply because crystallization is a process, not of art, but of the divine order of nature. Art can merely supply the conditions, but cannot impose the law, and the Creator has imposed the law on the cane-juice, and not on the corn-juice.

These illustrations may suffice to show the entire dependence of human art and skill on the infinite providence of God, — that providence which has sown in the bosom of creation the seeds of all uses and capabilities, whose harvest ripens along the ages under the same genial care which, in the briefer spaces of a simpler husbandry, renews the face of the earth, sends the early and the latter rain, and crowns the year with plenty.

I would next call your attention to the physical structure of man as specially adapted to the purposes of art. There are in one of our devotional hymns two lines peculiarly childish in sound, which yet contain the whole theory of civilization, and expound the earthly position and destiny of the human race. They are, —

> " Why was my body formed erect,
> While brutes bow down to earth ? "

Were it not for this simple difference, man might be possessed of all the native intellectual capacity he now has, and yet could gain scarcely any accurate knowledge of the universe, could embody his ideas only in the rudest forms, could transmit very little of his experience and wisdom or their results to future generations, and could bequeath to his immediate posterity hardly anything more precious than some savage booth or burrowing-place.

Man is perhaps the most feeble animal on earth in proportion to his size, yet he easily walks as sovereign, leads the behemoth in his train, tows the leviathan by his warp, makes the everlasting hills bow before him, lays his mandate and his chain on the giant forces of nature. And it is chiefly by means of the one divinely fashioned instrument, the hand, — through the elevation, expansion, and more complex organization of the very digits which we trace in less perfect development in the anterior limbs of every quadruped. The hand, — so slender and flexible that it might seem fitted neither for doing nor enduring, yet whose closely knit web-work of nerves and sinews concentrates the entire strength of the body, constituting a mightier force in proportion to its magnitude than is found in the whole universe beside; — the hand, combining all mechanical powers in one, — the fingers jointed levers, the sinews pulleys, whose elastic force is but imperfectly typified when by a series of artificial pulleys a slender silken thread is made to sustain as heavy a weight as a man could carry, the wrist-joint a perpetual screw without whose circular motion no screw of steel would ever find its way into its socket; — the hand, capable one moment of wielding a giant's strength, and the next of subserving the most delicate uses, dissecting the microscopic proportions of a flower-cup or an insect's wing, marking with the graver airlines subtile as the sunbeams, copying the vanishing hues of clouds and rosebuds and the human countenance, embodying thought in forms so ethereal that they might seem inbreathed by viewless spirits, rather than wrought by material agency, — the hand it is that makes man what he is, God's viceroy upon the earth. Reflect that there is no mechanical operation, whether of ruder craft or of the highest art, the capacity of which is not inherent in the hand, the direction of which is not one of the complex movements of which the hand is susceptible, the efficacy of which does not depend on the guidance or restraint of the hand. And what do we mean when we speak of water-power or steam-power taking the place of the hand? Simply this, — that, imperfectly copying some one or more of the countless number of divinely shaped instruments obtained by division or combination from our two wrist-joints and palms and our ten digits, we construct certain artificial hands, and then supply to them by the impetus of falling water or expanding steam the force which accrues from the principle of life to the nerves and sinews of the vital organism.

I have selected the hand as the prime executive member of the body, and I scarcely know of an object in the universe which so richly and beautifully manifests the Creator's wisdom, love, and providence, so that, were I obliged to confine myself to a single illustration, I would choose this before all others. But there is hardly one of the perceptive or active powers of the body which does not on analysis reveal kindred adaptations to industrial uses, showing that man brings into the world and carries through life fitnesses, capacities, and instrumentalities, which render art less his choice and achievement than a divinely imposed necessity of his nature.

Nor are these adaptations confined to the organs and faculties which we usually connect in our thought with industrial energy. They may be traced equally in the interior structure, in the vital organs and functions. Consider, for instance, the nutritive process in man. I look indeed with no complacency on the lot of the overtasked laborer, whether he be a slave by arbitrary law or by a no less tyrannical necessity, and I doubt not that in a future better than the present all labor will find its due meed of repose, relaxation, and space for the culture of the higher faculties. But thus far the requirements of human industry have demanded of the majority of mankind the constant and vigorous employment of the active powers through the greater part of every day; and it is believed that in no other animal does nutrition occupy and digestion appropriate to its own purposes so little time as in man. A single hour in the day might suffice for the taking of food (in our country many abridge even this scanty allotment, though not without injury or peril); and if food be taken in moderation, it may pass through all its essential stages without impeding the physical energy. Thus man may toil his ten or twelve hours daily with no cost to health or decline of strength. On the other hand, the ruminating animals demand for nutrition the greater part of their time, and are therefore incapable of anything approaching the vigorous and persistent bodily exertion necessary in many departments of human industry. The ox forms no exception. His strength, indeed, enables him to draw heavy weights; but he can be quickened only by cruelty, and then but for brief periods, beyond the naturally sluggish gait of his species. Nor does the sustained velocity of the camel, when we consider the length of his steps, bear any comparison to that persistent celerity of the human limbs which is essential alike to the more subtile processes and the immense aggregate of man's achievements in the industrial arts. Even the horse, man's most efficient helper, yields to him in the power of continuous effort. He needs so much time for feeding, that he is never capable of so many hours of unintermitted labor as man, and even in mere locomotion, it is well known that in a month or any long period of time a well-trained pedestrian will pass over more ground than the best-trained horse. You will perceive the pertinence of this comparison to the topic under discussion, when you reflect that there are not a few departments of human industry, and not infrequent industrial emergencies, in which persistency of labor is no less essential than artistical skill, and that this persistency is due, not to man's will or genius, but to the providence of the Creator, which has thus fitted him for his place and office as an industrial agent.

Again, it is man's boast that he can carry his industry and art over the whole world, and surround himself with their products in every climate. Let us look somewhat in detail at the providential element in this cosmopolitan adaptation, in which man stands alone among the inhabitants of the earth. It depends on the joint functions of circulation and respiration. In the severity of winter we may observe a strong contrast between different classes of the exposed. In the narrow streets and ill-built or poorly repaired houses of our towns and cities, we may find poverty-stricken families cowering with contracted limbs and chattering teeth over their scanty fires, while their dwellings often seem a mere lattice-work designed for the free passage of the northern blast. But with the thermometer at its lowest range, the woodman's axe plies with a vigorous and merry ring; the farmer trudges unchilled by the side of his team; and warm, glad life outspeeds the wind it braves in the swift sleighs that track our interior river-courses and lake-beds. The cause is manifestly internal, not external, — personal, not atmospheric. We are heated chiefly, not from without, but from within, — not by the fuel burned in our presence, but by the fuel which we ourselves consume. We carry about with us each his own hearth, with its vestal fire, — his own stove, with its perpetual radiation of heat. Our lungs are the seat of a constant combustion, literally of a coal-fire, kindled with our first breath, extinguished only with our last. The fuel is the carbon and hydrogen contained in our food, carried with other elements through the process of digestion and blood-making, conveyed to the lungs, and then oxidized, or, in other words, ignited and burned, by the oxygen inhaled from the atmosphere.

This process it is that heats the body, and at the same time resists to a certain, and in some cases to an almost incredible degree, the effect of external heat. In extreme cold no particle of blood remains near the surface for more than an instant; but the entire life-tide passes constantly to and from this central hearth, thus sending to the surface from moment to moment a freshly heated current. On the other hand, at an excessively high temperature, the ceaseless withdrawal of blood from the surface before it can become unduly heated preserves the internal temperature unchanged. This apparatus is imitated in that most effective mode of warming buildings, — a system of hot-water pipes, in which a heated and rarefied current of water sets constantly from the furnace or lungs to the remoter parts of the system, and a cooled and condensed current returns, as constantly, to be heated over again. By virtue of this arrangement in the human frame, a variation of more than two hundred degrees in external heat, from the drying-room or the mouth of a forge to the lowest Arctic temperature, occasions a difference of not more than three or four degrees in the human body.

Now the contrast between the suffering and the non-suffering in the severer exposures of our Northern climate is due to the different amounts of fuel employed to feed the internal flame. Fire, it is said, cannot warm the very poor, and this is because their meagre vegetable food, even if it seem unstinted, is deficient in carbon.

On the other hand, those who meet the bleakest exposures without suffering are well fed on carbon-yielding food, and the fire that they carry with them never burns low for lack of fuel. The perfect working of this apparatus has its best illustration in the experience of Dr. Kane and his companions. With a temperature sometimes of seventy degrees below zero, and for weeks together never rising above forty, often burrowing in the snow at these low temperatures, they found themselves more dependent on food than on fire. With an adequate supply of raw walrus meat and other unctuous, carbon-yielding food, they enjoyed health, comfort, vigor, gayety, hopefulness. When this supply fell short, the red-hot cabin stove seemed to yield no warmth, — nature drooped, sickened, and was ready to perish, reviving again, and glowing with its wonted fires, when a kind Providence again spread their board in proportion to their need.[1]

This self-heating apparatus has a most essential bearing on man's industrial capacity. By virtue of it he can toil at the forge and the furnace-mouth, and chase the whale and trap the seal in Polar seas; can say to the North, "Give up," and to the South, "Keep not back"; can bring together the fruits of every zone, and blend in the products of his industry the contributions of every soil and climate.

In man alone does this system attain a perfect adjustment. Other animals have their limits of latitude, some broader, some more restricted; none are cosmopolites. The camel and the reindeer could not change places.

---

[1] The reader can hardly fail to be reminded here that in high Arctic latitudes hardly any other than strongly unctuous food is attainable, and that of this, under ordinary circumstances, the natives are able to obtain an abundant supply.

The elephant could not winter in Greenland. The polar bear swelters under the tempered heat of one of our October days. Man alone can live and work wherever land, iceberg, or ocean gives him room to stand or float.

This vein of illustration might be followed much further; but I leave it, to develop a still more intimate relation between human art and the Creator. All art is mathematical. Thus music is equally with arithmetic a science of numbers; Pythagoras and Orpheus were equally identified with its early development; and it was better understood by Newton, La Grange, and Euler, than by Mozart, Beethoven, or Rossini. The problem of the flute-note is discussed in the Principia with the harmony of the spheres. The relative magnitude of the pipes of the organ, the length of their vibrations respectively, and the qualities of the resulting tones, form a series of numerical proportions no less definite and uniform than those which govern the planetary orbits; and the reason why the reed-pipes are oftener out of tune than the others is, that they involve complex problems which still lack a complete solution, so that the rules for their construction are but empirical. Musical intervals are rightly designated by numerical names, and might be as well represented on the score by numbers as by notes. Colors have their mathematical no less than their chemical laws, and, as they are separated by the prism or combined in art, they indicate relations which can be expressed only by abstract formulæ. Painting has no merit, unless the drawing be true, and all true drawing corresponds to one or another mode of mathematical projection. Architecture and mechanical operations of every kind depend on definite proportions, the violation of which can be compensated by no exuberance of beauty or misplaced accumulation of strength, but must issue in utter waste and ruin. Every department of engineering, the grading of the routes of travel, the construction of railways and bridges, the safety and efficiency of the water-wheel, the entire science of navigation, — all depend on mathematical laws coeval and coextensive with the universe, and navigation, on these laws as they span the solar system, and extend to stars whose distances elude calculation. The practical rules of even the inferior arts, the rules recognized by the laborer who knows not the multiplication-table, are derived from these world-embracing, universe-girdling laws. Were it not for the perception of these laws, we should still be at the lowest point of civilization. We should dare to rear only structures frail as a tent, or of ungainly and superfluous massiveness like the pyramids; no machine or mechanical power beyond a rude knife or mallet would help us in our toil; and our hollowed trunks of trees or bark canoes would still timidly skirt the seashore, and not venture beyond sight of land.

But the mathematical science in which art has its birth is literally a portion of the Divine mind. So far as we are cognizant of it, God gives us glimpses of the plan of the universe, permits us to handle the compasses with which he meted out the earth and spread the heavens, enables us to see precisely as he sees.

Here, then, is the highest dignity of art. It is the embodiment of absolute truth, the circumscription in material forms of universal and eternal laws, the transcript by human hands of the thoughts of God. Its rules could have been devised, codified, and applied only by minds that were taken up by the Creator into his own point of view, — taught by his inspiration the very relations and proportions that dwelt from all eternity in his omniscience, and were crystallized by his fiat in worlds, suns, and systems.

We have now reached the climax of human art. Man disappears, and what he calls his work is but the manifestation of the one creative, all-pervading Spirit, — great and glorious in the massive and sky-reaching structures of human genius, in the world-subduing energies of science, in the thronged marts of industry and traffic, no less than in the silent mountain, the primeval forest, or the many-twinkling smile and the multitudinous roar of the ocean-waves.

While the discussion in which I have led you this evening has its fitting and almost necessary place in a course of Lectures on natural religion, I am the more glad to lead you over this ground, because the tendency of our times is, I might almost say, to art-worship, — to the sentiment which had its type and reached its culminating-point in the ancient monarch, when he said, "Is not this great Babylon that I have built, by the might of my power and for the honor of my majesty?" Much of the practical skill, mechanical genius, and executive capacity of the day is materialistic, — Titanic alike in its strength and its impiety, worshipping only its own capacity and its master-workmen. The rapidity and vastness of man's aggressions upon nature, the iron girdles with which he clasps the continent, the lightnings that bear his mandates from zone to zone, are constantly dwelt upon, not as outgoings of Omnipotent Wisdom, but as the apotheosis of art and science, and the great discoverers, inventors, and mechanicians of the age have honors rendered to them hardly less than divine. Meanwhile the sacred solitudes where holy men were wont to commune in silence with the Almighty are solitudes no longer. Art obtrudes her forces where once were secluded shrines of natural grandeur and beauty, lays her iron track across the sunless ravines, wakes with the shout and tramp of her cars the echoes of the ancient hills.

I have endeavored to show you that these works of man are in a higher and more intimate sense the works of God, — that in all in which man seeks his own glory he but manifests the glory of the Creator. "Let the people praise thee, O God, yea, let all the people praise thee." The views that I have presented blend in worship the tribute of art with the spontaneous incense that floats in temples on which there has been no sound of axe or hammer, — compels the throng and tide of toiling hands and throbbing brains and reasoning minds to take up the strain of universal nature, the song of angels and of ransomed men : — " Great and marvellous are thy works, Lord God Almighty, — great where thy hand hath wrought in everlasting silence, no less marvellous where thine inspiration hath guided, thy might strengthened, thy loving providence crowned, the work of thy children upon earth."

LECTURE VII.

THE PROVIDENCE OF GOD IN HUMAN SOCIETY.

My last Lecture related to the Divine Providence in art. I propose this evening to consider that same Providence as manifested in the diversity of native endowments, capacities, and tendencies among the races of men and among individuals of the same race.

The Scriptural idea of mankind is that of unity in diversity, — one body, many members, — the same spirit, diverse gifts and administrations, — one God, who worketh all in all, but who distributes talents and capabilities with reference not alone to individual well-being, but equally to the common good. The *solidarity* of the race, so far from being a modern idea, has the most complete statement of it that was ever made in the twelfth chapter of St. Paul's First Epistle to the Corinthians, and crops out, as one of his favorite conceptions, in numerous passages of his other Epistles. What more perfect expression of it can human language admit of, than when, making Christ the head, he adds: "From whom the whole body, fitly joined together, and compacted from that which every joint supplieth, according to the effectual working of the measure in every part, maketh increase of the body to the edifying of itself in love"?

Let us see how this idea verifies itself in the actual condition of mankind. We will look first at the several races of men. Nothing can be more obvious than the indelibleness of national characteristics. Barbarism does not obliterate them, nor does the highest cultivation supplant them. The types may be improved or deteriorated, but they always remain distinct. The Jew is a Jew all the world over, and as much so now that he has had no country of his own for nearly eighteen centuries, as when Jerusalem was in its glory. The Greeks have retained their love of nature and of art through ages of depression and enslavement.

> "On Suli's rock and Parga's shore
> Exist the remnants of a line
> Such as the Doric mothers bore,"

and the nation is awaking from its slumber with the very same salient features which we trace in the Periclean era. The Hindoo, though imbued with all the literature and wisdom of Europe, still retains his Asiatic cast of mind and stamp of character; while Europeans may live generation after generation in Hindostan or in China without becoming Orientalized, and may found and people colonies in every zone without any essential change of the traits that distinguished them in the countries whence they came. These things premised, we will now, to illustrate the *solidarity* of the human family in the differences of the races, consider the Caucasian, the Asiatic, and the African groups of nations respectively, — a division by no means exhausting or scientifically exact, yet sufficiently so for the use I propose to make of it.

The Caucasian race, wherever found, holds the foremost place as to the cognitive and reasoning faculties, strength of will, love of power, and executive energy. These qualities have, indeed, been kept in abeyance during portions of the history of some nations, through the repressive force of religious superstition or of governmental oppression; but there is no one of the group that has not at some period manifested them, and that would not be expected to manifest them were the limiting circumstances partially removed. They seem born rulers and lawgivers, are impatient of restraint, uneasy subjects of arbitrary sway, and incapable of being permanently enslaved or subdued. They have the clear, scientific eye, the power and habit of ratiocination, an indisposition to take truth on trust, an aptness for investigation, research, and discovery. They have furnished all the great inventors of the race, if we except those that must at some remote epoch have flourished among the Chinese and Japanese, from whom they differ in the vigorous and rapid progress of their art, while among the Eastern nations art is stationary, and its processes slow, conducted with little aid from machinery, and with an indisposition to learn new and improved methods. But with the Caucasian races, the imagination follows in the wake of reason, intuition lags behind demonstration, and the affections, instead of giving law, are in subjection to the intellectual nature.

The Asiatic mind is easily swayed by impressions from without, in close sympathy with nature, keenly sensitive to its beauties and its harmonies, full of gorgeous fancies, rich in poetic elements, kaleidoscopic in the profusion, variety, and splendor of its imaginative literature. But it is slow to reason, it has neither prudence nor persistency in counsel, and its affections are subordinated to the imagination.

The African races, with all their depression, still show in some directions superior capacity. Docility, obedience, and love are their native traits, — traits not developed by their long servitude, but essential to render their enslavement possible; for the experiment of enslaving other races has been repeatedly tried, but has never permanently succeeded. The Africans often submit to their bondage, with full consciousness of their wrongs and of their power to resent them, by virtue of a moral instinct averse from violence, and willing to endure oppression rather than to avenge it. Whatever culture they receive goes at once to the affections, — takes a moral and religious direction. To educate them is, with rare exceptions, to make them devout, grateful, kind, and exemplary in their social relations and duties. With the highest culture that they can attain, it is doubtful whether they will ever excel in science, art, or poetry, or will furnish any considerable proportion of commanding, cogent minds. But there is every reason to believe that they may be so trained as to exhibit the richest traits of moral excellence, to be the ready recipients of the highest social influences, and to reflect the love, as other races reflect the wisdom and beauty, of the Creator.

The relations of these several races are now deranged, and their mutual correspondences obscured, by the presence of moral evil. The Caucasian, in the pride of his strength, makes the Asiatic his tributary, the African his slave, and, in his insatiable lust for power and territory, is always ready to convert the earth into an Aceldama and a Golgotha. Thus reason and will usurp the supremacy over the gentler elements of character, and mutual alienation — contempt and fear, violence and wrong-suffering — prevents the nations from recognizing in one another the traits of the godlike which each might admire and copy in every other. But let the ages roll on, and, while science and skill weave their network of ever closer material communion and interest, let the gospel of brotherhood clasp its zone around the nations, and put a period to war, slavery, and oppression, — then may not the differences of the races blend in the most perfect and beautiful harmony? May not each from its peculiar vein contribute equally to the joint stock of elevating and refining influences? May not each be at once the source and the recipient of sentiments and impulses, without which neither can fill its place and discharge its mission? Will not reason own the transcendent loveliness of the affections, and they in their turn do homage to the majesty of reason, and fancy, while it breathes poetry into science and shapes the paradise of love, seek where it bestows, and draw truth and fervor from the very fountains into which it pours its own exuberant wealth of beauty? Thus in coming ages will the whole human family combine to constitute the second Adam, myriad-formed, bearing every capacity and perfection that the first Adam might have developed had he remained sinless in Eden. Thus will the immeasurable Creator see the whole circle of his attributes reflected from the face of humanity with a resplendence infinitely brighter than can ever be mirrored in the material universe, or has been beheld in the human form except in Him alone who in the form of man outrayed the brightness of the Father's glory. The development of these harmonies may be yet far distant; but in the capacity for them which our race manifests in its present blindness and perversion, in the tendency to them which we discern through all the darkness and misery that brood over the earth, we mark the tokens of a far-seeing providence, which we can trace back through all the ages of authentic history, and thus, with undoubting faith, on through an ever-brightening future.

From this broad view let us now pass to the distribution of talents among persons of the same age and nation. Here it cannot be needful to defend the position, that the differences of ability are in great part native, not acquired; — that genius and talent, so far from being the result of education or of favoring circumstances, will work their way through obstacles that seem insurmountable, and will make any posture of circumstances propitious to their own development; while many persons who would gladly distinguish themselves in particular departments, who do all that they can do, and are helped by others so far as help can be made availing, hardly reach mediocrity. This diversity of natural gifts is so almost universally admitted, that any argument in its favor would seem lost labor. Taking it, then, for granted, we will proceed to consider the Divine providence in their distribution.

Writers on natural religion are wont to infer the wisdom and goodness of the Creator from the distribution of land and water, of wood, salt, coal, and metals, in fine, of all the materials of man's outward well-being, in such a way that the relation of demand and supply can never suffer any serious derangement. The same relation of demand and supply prevails in man's native endowments and capacities. Talents are bestowed as they are needed and can be used, with that liberal frugality, that measured generosity, which enhances the value of all God's higher gifts, and attests the careful economy of the Giver.

The only universal need is that of moral goodness; and of this the capacity is universal, except in the rare case of mental disease; while (as I shall show hereafter) the humblest intellectual endowments do not preclude one even from eminence in goodness. For hand-labor and mechanical operations a very large supply of human strength and skill is always needed, and, to meet this need, the great majority of men are so constituted as to be fitted for such departments of industry, to find improvement and happiness in them, and, with other walks of life in full view, to be conscious neither of desire nor of adaptation for a different sphere. Then there is needed a certain proportion of men capable of conducting combined industry and extended enterprise, of directing the skill and employing the labor of others, and of distributing and exchanging the products of agriculture and handcraft. It is a patent fact that these departments of business are sadly overcrowded; but the multitude of those who cannot by any training be moulded into a capacity for them, and who flounder on through successive failures from a sanguine youth to a poverty-stricken old age, authorizes the belief that the Creator has fitted for these duties no more than the world needs.

We verify the same law of distribution in social and political relations. Of minds capable of leading and controlling the action of other minds, bearing the signature of native supremacy, endowed with the legitimate right and power of influence, there are enough, yet not more than enough, to serve as interpreters of truth and duty, counsellors, judges, magistrates, and legislators. Nor is this proportion essentially modified by the institutions of society. It is as large among savage as among civilized nations; it furnishes the same relative quota of leaders and sages for the council-fire in the wigwam as for the senate or the parliament. Arbitrary forms of government do not diminish the number of these controlling minds, though, when crowded out of their appropriate spheres, they either, as in modern Germany, waste themselves in fruitless activity, becoming poets without inspiration, authors without taste or tact, supernumeraries in departments of literature and research that demand a widely different order of intellect, or, as in Italy, they employ their genius in undermining the institutions of which they are the natural conservators and administrators. Nor does a democratic *régime*, as it is sometimes idly asserted, multiply talents of this class; but when offices outnumber the needs of the people, are created for party purposes, and sought for their spoils, for lack of fit candidates they must be filled by men destitute of the capacity to counsel, legislate, rule, or judge.

To pass to the realm of literature and art, the poet is born, not made. If he could be made by mere endeavor or practice, there would be as many poets as readers; for the habit of rhyming is contracted at some period by almost every person that can write, and is persisted in through life by very many. Yet of poets by birthright and the gift of God there are exceedingly few in any one generation, in some scarce any, though on the muster-roll of all ages and lands they constitute no mean array, and are sufficiently various and divergent in style and subject to meet every hue and grade of taste, and to furnish every description of demand. Were the poets still fewer, their works would be inaccessible to many capable of enjoying them to the full, and some veins of true poetic sentiment would be overlooked, some tastes unprovided for. Were they more numerous, the fruits of their genius would be less precious, less enjoyed, less prized, and the world, flooded with true poetry, as now with its counterfeit, would lose the power of appreciation.

Here I would have you remark the rigid, merciful, and beautiful parsimony which, in all the higher departments of art and literature, governs the proportion between power and taste, genius and susceptibility, — between those who create and those who can enjoy and appreciate. In these departments one can minister to the pleasure and profit of hundreds, thousands, communities, nations; and, accordingly, to one capable of thus ministering, there are multitudes that can avail themselves of his ministry. Of all the higher forms of art, the most common is oratory, — that is, the capacity of kindling, swaying, convincing, persuading, gladdening gathered crowds by the vivid presentation, in word and gesture, of thoughts and sentiments capable of powerfully interesting and moving the judgment and the emotional nature. This gift is sufficiently common to bring all occasionally within the sphere of its exercise, yet sufficiently rare to make that exercise an uncloying and unwearying joy to the hearers. But of true orators a large proportion succeed by virtue of endowments evanescent in their nature, and have not the higher power of clothing their burning thoughts in words that can retain their prestige beyond reach of the living voice; for authors are much fewer than orators. The capacity of successful authorship, immeasurably rarer than the endeavor, is yet frequent enough for the needs of the reading public, even were education universal; but among those who can read with discrimination, pleasure, and profit the records of fancy, wit, or wisdom, there is not one in ten thousand whom any possible training could have made the writer of books that would live and last. In the plastic arts, of artists worthy of the name, or of those who by any possibility could have become such, there are very few. Were there more, their creations would cease to be valued and to give pleasure. There are enough, and no more than enough, to minister to the taste of the thousands and millions who can be gladdened, improved, refined, and elevated by their works. Of musical composers, actual and potential, there are enough, yet not more than enough, to furnish compass and variety for the incessant demand made for social, festive, and religious uses. Skilful musical performers, also, are to be everywhere found in sufficient number for the solace, delight, and edification of all who rejoice in the concord of sweet sounds. Yet the most diligent use of the Pestalozzian system, the most assiduous drilling of the infant ear and voice, falls far short of developing the predicted universality of musical talent, which we might well deprecate — had not a kind Providence set up impassable barriers against it — as rendering the art cheap, paltry, and worthless. Let training-schools of music be established in every hamlet, let musical instruction be proffered to every pupil in all our seminaries of learning, from the Kindergarten to the college, let a piano find shelter under every roof, — still the proportion of those who can yield delight by musical performance to those who can enjoy, and in some good measure appreciate, the achievements of musical skill and genius, must ever remain small.

In the distribution of natural endowments which I have now exhibited there are several points worthy of emphatic consideration. 1. The higher tastes, the intellectual demands, of the vast majority of mankind are fully met without their being taken from the walks of productive industry. They can enjoy all the pleasure and all the mental emolument of art, literature, and poetry, through labor, self-discipline, and self-sacrifice in which they have borne no part. 2. The classes of talent which are developed the most slowly and laboriously are distributed the most sparingly, and are at the same time endowed with an extent of influence commensurate with the outlay of time and effort in their cultivation. 3. In proportion to the difficulties to be overcome, the toil to be performed, the sacrifice to be borne, in the cultivation of any class of talents, is its power of self-diffusion in space and time. Thus the poet or the artist of the highest type, made what he is only by stern self-denial and rigid self-discipline, gives his name to his age, transmits his memory to all succeeding centuries, and is compensated for toil and straitness by the assurance that his works will live in distant generations, and that his genius will be recognized and felt throughout the civilized world.

Does not the distribution of natural endowments, thus symmetrical and mutually self-compensating, manifest a presiding Providence, if possible, even more fully than analogous arrangements in the outward creation? We here see that the principle of the division of labor, which has been represented as the great industrial device of modern times, by which alone skill can be perfected and its highest productiveness insured, is distinctly recognized by the Supreme Being in the order and economy of the creation, so that in this regard man is but copying the Divine precedent and pattern. You will remember that in my last Lecture I showed you how the highest art constantly resolves itself into the imitation of the Creator. The case is precisely the same in social and political economy, which, when not false and mischievous, is little else than the application — often unconscious — to particular communities and organizations of the methods of the Divine providence, so that we might reverently employ concerning whatever is wise and salutary in the institutions of all God's human children the words in which Jesus characterizes his miracles: "The Son can do nothing of himself, but what he seeth the Father do."

But while as an economical arrangement this distribution of talents satisfies the taste and judgment, certainly of those who account themselves as among the more favored, it needs to be further illustrated, and even claims defence, in the case of those who occupy what is deemed the lowest place in the scale of Divine allotments. In a former Lecture I considered the condition of those destitute of moral and religious privilege; I now ask you to look with me at the case of those who, in the established order of civilized society, would be termed unprivileged, — the laborers, the proletaries, the many who seem doomed to incessant toil and burden for the luxury of the few. If they are by virtue of their occupation shut out from the benefits and blessings which should appertain to them as intellectual and moral beings, if they are of necessity devoid of privilege, then, though the plan of the Divine administration which we have been reviewing may illustrate the wisdom, it throws doubt on the love, of the Creator. But if we find that they are adequately cared for, the argument for a Providence no less merciful than wise remains untouched. Let us try this issue.

In the first place, labor is not of necessity unfavorable to mental or moral development. Even in its most complex forms it easily becomes so much a matter of routine as to leave the thoughts free. The mind can in the humblest sphere find ample materials for reflection and means of improvement, while the kindly and devout affections may be cherished, and all the essential duties of the soul's life discharged, in a position however obscure and toilsome. Vigorous minds, distinctly cognizant of everything within their natural range of knowledge,' are as often and as symmetrically formed in the laborious walks of life, as in those styled peculiarly intellectual. Both in England and in America, many have passed from the last and the loom to conspicuous places in literature and in public life, by virtue of mental acumen and vigor largely developed before they stinted the full measure of their daily labor. And how many there are, that never leave the work-bench or the plough, who are shrewd, sagacious, endowed with sterling good-sense, possessed of large practical wisdom, skilful in judging of character, weighing arguments, and testing evidence! How many too, who have manifested the loftiest moral traits, and from whose stores of ethical and religious knowledge Socrates and Plato would have deemed themselves privileged learners! What greater man, in that wisdom which adapts means to ends, in that saintly wisdom which adapts the choicest means to the noblest ends, has the present century seen, than John Pounds, the cobbler? He entered on his life of unceasing toil with much less than a New England common-school education. He never learned to *make* a shoe, and in his nearly fourscore years he performed as large an amount of minute and grovelling task-work as any man in Great Britain. Yet he found time and mind and heart to rescue from ruin, and to raise to his own humble level in social life, and toward his own exalted rank in the moral hierarchy, several hundreds of orphaned and neglected children about the lanes and wharves of his native city, and to win for himself an enduring name among the first philanthropists in the world's annals.

The mention of John Pounds reminds me of the fraternity of St. Crispin, in both hemispheres, which has almost vindicated for itself a place among the liberal professions by its high grade of general intelligence, and by the number of eminent men who have issued from its ranks, from Hans Sachs, whose lyrics were among the great forces of the Protestant Reformation, to our own Whittier, whose place in the foremost rank of living poets none can challenge. Who work harder than the shoemakers of Massachusetts? Yet in what class of men is there more general activity of intellect, not to speak of the numerous instances in which the irrepressible force of genius has elevated members of their brotherhood to the highest eminence at the bar, in the pulpit, in the counsels of the State and nation? Surely labor is not unprivileged.

But though a life of incessant labor does not preclude the education of the higher nature, it is beginning to be admitted on all hands that neither does the order of Providence require, nor can the general welfare permit, such a life to be the destiny of any portion of our race. Man is overworked as regards the needs of humanity. Excessive production is the most fruitful source of commercial convulsions, financial derangements, and of penury and starvation among the laboring classes. But reserving this point for future discussion, and supposing that all the work that is done is needed, it is performed by much fewer laborers than ought to be engaged in it. Vast numbers properly belonging to the ranks of productive industry forsake them, or are forced out of them, and if they remained, they would greatly diminish the amount of toil *per capita*. There are multitudes constantly pressing into commercial life, without talent or education for business, with no possibility of success, without even elbow-room in the crowd of competitors. Then there are the wasteful armies and navies of the Old World and the New, — generally worse than useless,[1] — converting their myriads of potential producers into unproductive consumers.

Consider also how large a proportion of the products of the earth is perverted from nourishment into poison. An immense percentage of the sugar and grain crops goes into market only in the form of alcoholic liquors, which in small part are made availing for medicinal and industrial uses, but for the most part are worse than wasted, and are the most potent of all agencies in reducing the working force of humanity.

With these allowances for laborers abstracted and labor wasted, the handcraft of Christendom, when in full employ, gluts every market, and heaps up masses of commodities of every kind in the hands of dealers. Then prices fall ruinously low, manufactories suspend operations, farmers till less land, laborers are thrown out of employment by the thousand, and industry suffers a paralysis, till the supply is reduced, and a fresh demand raises prices and stimulates enterprise anew. All this indicates that, with the industrial machinery in full operation, more work is done than man needs to have done.

---

[1] The writer will not of course be understood as applying the epithet "worse than useless" to the forces now or at any time employed in protecting the fundamental law and the essential institutions of the state, in guarding its frontiers from actual peril, or in preventing depredations upon its commerce on the seas. But in time of peace, a very large portion of the military and naval force in commission and pay in the various countries of Christendom not only serves no immediate purpose of defence or protection, but is not even in readiness for such service, an army or navy at the commencement of a war always evincing full as much need of being purged of inefficient officers and men, as of new enlistments.

If, when men work twelve or fourteen hours a day, a large proportion of the laborers must lie idle one year out of every four or five, to keep the supply of the commodities within reach of the demand, the same end would be more conveniently brought about by their working but nine or ten hours a day, and having constant employment. Nor could the laborer lose, nay, he would rather gain, in wages by the general shortening of his day's work. His wages are not governed by the value he creates; for labor creates all value, pays all income and revenue. Every dollar of the millionnaire's dividends is ploughed for, and delved for, and hammered for. The entire capital of the community, in order to be productive, must pass through the various channels of handcraft. The laborer's share of what he earns depends, on the one hand, on his own intelligence, self-respect, moral worth, and appreciation of the comforts and refinements of civilized life, and, on the other hand, on his employer's sense of justice. If he toil unremittingly, and have no space for the culture of the higher traits of mind and character, he will be compensated on the lowest scale of his absolute necessity; for he will be too ignorant, thriftless, and reckless to claim more, and he will not command sufficient respect to have more awarded to him. But if by a less amount of toil he yet produce his fair quota toward a supply of the wants of the community, he can, by the cultivation of mind and heart, place himself on the same moral level with his employer, — his demands will rise with his conscious needs, his wages will grow with the growth of his substantial claims to respect and deference, and he will be allowed his just dividend of the annual revenue of his labor; while the enterprise that employs, the skill that directs, and the capital that sustains his industry will receive their equitable proportion, and no more.

The working of this principle has been tested by the general establishment of the ten-hour system in some departments of industry. The operatives in these departments are better paid than before; employers have felt no injustice; and in the increased intelligence and respectability of the employed, and in the diminished tendency to overworking at some periods, and to a consequent glut of the labor-market at frequent intervals, the relations of capital and industry, and of demand and supply, have become more stable, and approached a more equable adjustment. The operation of this same principle must soon extend itself to all departments of industry. It cannot be hastened by agitation or by factious combination, which only excites resistance and arrays public opinion on the wrong side. It will gradually establish itself with the recognition of sound views of social economy, of the republican doctrine of equal rights, and of mutual justice between man and man. The time cannot be far distant when, in New England at least, the disastrous system of overworking and overproduction will be permanently set aside, and the hours and amount of regular labor will be so adjusted to the actual needs of home and foreign markets, as to prevent the spasms of consuming toil and intervals of hungry idleness which have hitherto alternated in the history of the industrial world.

We are at present concerned with the fundamental laws of the Divine Providence, not with artificial arrangements in contravention of those laws. I have shown you that one of those laws is, that much less than the incessant toil of the laboring classes will produce all that man requires for subsistence, comfort, and luxury. Consequently, Providence has indicated for the laborer ample season for relaxation and improvement.

In a state of society conformed to its essential laws, no day would pass for any member of the community in exhausting toil,—every day would have its leisure hours for domestic enjoyment, for the culture of the mental powers, and for the indulgence of refined tastes. Thus, by the universal diffusion of the elevating influences of leisure and prosperity, the artificial distinctions of society would fall away; all occupations would become liberal professions; the man in every case would ennoble his calling and reflect honor upon it; and all the essential offices of life would be discharged without menial or degrading associations attaching themselves to any, because he who performed even the humblest function, instead of being wholly merged in it, would have existence and time, a *status*, an intellectual, moral, and social life, independent of it.

In even pace with this tendency toward a high general level of social life, the civilized world must approach nearer an equal distribution of material wealth. Not only will capital earn less and labor more; but with the general diffusion of intelligence and the enhanced compensation of labor the number of small capitalists will be constantly on the increase, and the union of capital and labor will become general. To be sure, there must always be considerable accumulations of capital. They are demanded for the general good, as safety-funds and movement-funds. The surface of society must always be diversified. But there is no need of Alpine scenery,—riches piled mountain high, with sunless and barren ravines in the chasms. Far better is it that hill and valley should alike lie under the common sunlight, and equally wave with harvest wealth.

There is yet one point more with reference to the

elevation of labor, which I want to illustrate. I exhibited to you in my last Lecture the Divine Providence in Art. Of this providence the chief revenue accrues to the laborer. Invention, machinery, steam, magnetism, all are especially for his emolument. Without them, the heirs of great names and ancestral acres would live in rude plenty and barbaric splendor, would lack nothing which they could appreciate, and by their monopoly of land — the only source of wealth — would keep the laboring classes in a dependent and needy serfdom. But machinery creates a wealth that cannot be monopolized. A labor-saving invention confers a permanent estate or settles an annual revenue on each of the laborers of the country where it is used, and even of the civilized world. Take, for instance, an invention by which two men can do the work which ten used to do, and suppose it applied to a department of labor in which ten thousand men have been employed. It is manifest that the labor of eight thousand men can be dispensed with, and the amount of production remain the same as before. Now if these eight thousand men were dismissed summarily from employment, the result would be a burden, and not a blessing, to the community. But this is not the case. In all probability they will remain in the business, and aid in producing five times as much of the commodity as was produced before; for, by dispensing with four fifths of the labor, the commodity is cheapened to two thirds, one half, or even one third of its former price, and consequently many can afford to use it who never used it before, and many with whom it was before a luxury or a rarity can now make free and common use of it. Thus the products of the labor of these eight thousand men, being four times as much of the commodity in question as was previously manufactured, are thrown into the cheap market, chiefly for the benefit of the laboring classes, — of men who must wait till a commodity is cheap, in order to purchase it freely, if at all. If it be cotton cloth or calico, they can dress their families with a neatness and comfort not before attainable. If it be glass or porcelain, they can gratify their taste in their table furniture. If it be paper, they can indulge themselves and their children with an occasional new book or a daily journal. If it be an article not unproductively consumed, but used for the production of other goods, they derive the same advantage in the cheaper rate at which those goods are procured. If the commodity be one adapted to general use, probably not only the eight thousand will remain in the manufacture, but the demand will grow so fast as to create a considerable indraft from the labor-market at large, and thus to enhance in some measure the average rate of wages. And let it be borne in mind that the increased consumption is, almost all of it, by the poorer classes, — by the laborers. Rich men used as much as they wanted of the commodity thus multiplied, at the higher prices; the invention benefits those who could not previously afford to purchase it.

I have said that in this supposed case the labor of the eight thousand men is a gift of Providence to the laboring portion of the community. But there are two forms in which they may take the gift. They may take it in goods, as I have already shown you, or they may take it in time, by the absorption of the disengaged eight thousand into the general mass of laborers, the same amount of production being accomplished as before, but by fewer hours of labor on the part of each operative of every class. The gift has in fact been accepted in both forms; thus far, how ever, principally in the former, while in coming generations it will no doubt be oftener welcomed in the latter. It has been hitherto taken chiefly in goods, because so many desirable articles of comfort and enjoyment have been made easily accessible and temptingly cheap. The advance in the condition of the laboring classes within half a century is almost fabulous. The man who unites industry with a moderate degree of skill lacks hardly anything that could make him happier. As to the essentials of comfort, the levelling upward, except among the indolent, thriftless, and vicious, has reached a higher grade than Utopians would have dreamed two or three generations ago. And now that laborers have received, in goods, nearly as much of the revenue which comes to them from machinery as they desire to receive in that form, they are turning their attention to the matter of time, and claiming a part of their dividend in hours, — in leisure to enjoy the homes that have been made so comfortable, the added measure of goods that has fallen to their inheritance. Invention and machinery, having been first made efficient in multiplying comforts and luxuries, will now go on to accomplish their mission in emancipating the laborer from continuous toil, by enabling the laboring force of the world to do all the world's work within hours that shall impose no heavy burden or depressing weariness, and shall leave the paths of higher culture and superior privilege as freely open to those who are distinctively workers, as to those who dignify their lives by the name of some liberal profession.

I have thus shown you, with reference to those who, in our social system, seem to have the least of privilege, — first, that, in the order of Providence, the time spent in labor is not lost to higher purposes; secondly, that more work is now done, when industrial agencies are in full operation, than the race needs; and, thirdly, that, in the progress of inventive art, there is ample provision for the material comfort, the abundant leisure, and the high mental, moral, and spiritual culture of the laborers, — all which, be it remembered, is not the growth of man's philanthropy (for man has done next to nothing on a large scale for his fellow-man), but the development of the counsels of Him, of whom revelation tells us that his tender mercies are over all his works, and his loving-kindness unto all the children of men.

LECTURE VIII.

THE HOLINESS OF GOD. — GOD IN CHRIST.

In a previous Lecture I named goodness and holiness as the two principal aspects of the Divine character presented by Christianity. I have thus far spoken of the first of these only, as confirmed and illustrated by the religion of nature. I now ask your attention to the second, which will occupy the earlier portion of the present hour.

Holiness primarily denotes *wholeness*, and, as applied to character, it indicates perfect purity, any lack of purity being a defect, and thus detracting from the wholeness of character. The natural and necessary manifestation of holiness in God is a supreme reference to moral distinctions in the structure and government of the universe. Let us see how far it is so manifested as to claim for it a place among the truths of natural religion.

I. It is manifested in the human conscience. What is conscience? It is the internal perception corresponding to the word *ought*, which denotes *owed* or *obligated*. And why ought I to do this or that? Because it is intrinsically right, in accordance with the nature of things, in harmony with an eternal law which I can neither set aside nor evade. This sense of obligation, with the correlative sense of right, is native, intuitive. It exists in the very dawn of the moral nature. We cannot remember the time when we had it not. We trace it in the infant as early as we can trace anything beyond sensation. It is not the result of education, but the basis of education. The parent does not awaken it, but appeals to it in the earliest forms and acts of moral discipline. It can no more be expelled or escaped from, than can the consciousness of existence.

Conscience is unerring. The conviction *I ought* is never felt with reference to anything but that which is intrinsically, necessarily, eternally right. There are, indeed, many cases of conscientious wrong-doing; but how? Not through a perverted sense of right, but through imperfect knowledge or defective judgment as to the proper means of actualizing the sense of right. In conscientious wrong-doing the *animus* of the act is right; the thing done is what in the abstract ought to be done; there is merely a mistake as to the method in which the honest, benevolent, or devout purpose may be fitly carried into effect, that is, a mistake, not as to one's own obligation, but as to beings, objects, and relations external to himself. Thus the conscientious persecutor of those whom he deems heretics is right in believing that he ought to sacrifice every inferior consideration to the reverence and worship of God; wrong only in supposing that the property, liberty, and lives of his fellow-citizens are his for the purpose of sacrifice. Thus, also, the absurdities and extravagances of fanaticism are expressions of that loyalty to God in which all moral good has its source and its end; the mistake is solely one of taste and judgment, as to the exterior becomingness and utility of certain modes of expressing the loyalty of the heart, — modes in themselves innocent, and which would be as becoming and useful as any other modes, were they not inconsistent with conventional propriety. Conscience never sanctions a wrong *disposition, motive,* or *feeling;* but its province lies wholly within, — the mode in which it shall embody itself is a subject for legislation, human or Divine. When the law prescribes only outward acts in themselves right or indifferent, conscience takes the law as she finds it. But when legislation lays sacrilegious hands on the ark of God in the soul, invades the realm of conscience, commands what she forbids, or forbids what she commands, the law is paralyzed before the divine majesty of right. It may make submissive martyrs, whose blood shall cry out of the ground for its repeal; but it can no more depose conscience from her judgment-seat than it can usurp the throne of the universe.

I have said that the office of conscience is involved in the word *ought,* — *owed.* But the *ought* must have its object. It implies a double personality, — the person owing, and the person to whom the obligation is due. It has not a merely human reference; for it adheres to portions of our lives in which we can have no human creditor, in which our fellow-beings have no interest, — to thoughts and feelings which they cannot even know. When I say *I ought,* I confess myself amenable to God; I acknowledge that I owe to him thoughts, words, and deeds conformed to his will, deserving his approval, nay, more, accordant with his nature; for his will must be the expression of his nature, and if he wills purity, truth, and love, it must be because he is stainlessly pure, eternally true, infinitely good.

Still further, conscience is not only the reflection of the Divine nature, — it is, not in metaphor, but in literal fact, the God within. Man constantly errs; conscience is infallible. Man changes from youth to age, from generation to generation; conscience is unchangeable. Man is tempted; conscience knows no bribe. Man may make himself utterly vile; but in the entire wreck and ruin of his nature conscience is as loyal to the right in plying its scourge of scorpions, as when it echoes the plaudit of a justifying God on a life nobly spent or nobly sacrificed.

God is everywhere. He is present in inanimate nature in those laws which are his unceasing fiat. He is present with the brute creation in instinct, through whose impulse the unreasoning races fulfil his bidding. He is present with men in conscience. And as without his presence in nature the forms of the visible creation would collapse and perish; as without his presence in instinct the tribes of air, land, and sea would rush to ruin; so without his presence in conscience the bonds of society would be sundered, government would be impossible, natural affection would be turned to hatred, and our whole race would be blended in a tumultuous warfare of mutual destruction.

In saying this, I am aware that I ascribe to conscience a degree of influence over society as it now is, which is not generally recognized. But with all the wrong-doing that there is among men, the overwhelming majority of the individual acts performed in the world are not only right and good, but strictly conscientious acts; and even the very worst men are generally conscientious, except as to those particulars of conduct in which their ruling appetite or passion is immediately concerned. Go as low as you will in the scale of moral turpitude, you still do not find utter indifference to moral distinctions. I doubt whether there lives a sane man who, when selfish motives are equally balanced between the right and the wrong, would not choose the right, though he might not know why,— by an inward movement closely analogous to that which leads the brute to elect wholesome and to shun unwholesome food. It is on the ground of this innate and never inactive sense of right that, if you know a bad man, you may calculate the veins in which his vicious propensities will run; and can generally trust him in every other direction.

In fine, a large proportion of the trust which we think we repose in one another, is not trust in man, but trust in God as he is present with man in the indestructible conscience. The man who would rob you if he met you in a secluded spot, is more likely than not to show you gratuitous kindness, if the opportunity of gratifying his cupidity be wanting. You are on a perplexing journey, and, without thought of his moral condition, you confidently ask information of the first man you meet. He may be a person of the most depraved character, yet, if he has no motive for misleading you, you know that you can depend on what he tells you. You are ill among strangers, and very probably you will have for your unasked and most assiduous attendants and helpers persons who in certain ways are the slaves of evil appetites or passions. In truth, men never sin untempted, and they generally do right and good when there is no selfish motive to evil.

Nay, more. You often witness great virtues in connection with gross defects and faults, — sincere patriotism where the private morality bears a low stamp, private excellence combined with political profligacy, honesty in the sensualist, benevolence among the intemperate, domestic fidelity among those whose uprightness in business relations you cannot trust. To be sure, the character which in any one respect is faulty is weaker at other points than if it were without stain, — is more liable to yield to new forms of temptation; yet, under ordinary circumstances, a man who is, in the common phrase, destitute of principle, may be relied on for the continued performance of the good which he has been accustomed to do, no less than he may be expected still to yield, whenever occasion presents itself, to his easily-besetting frailties and sins. And thus, as I have said, the overwhelming majority of the acts performed are right and good, salutary and helpful.

But here let me make a most emphatic distinction. I cannot regard this spontaneous goodness as worthy of moral approbation, which he alone deserves who can resist temptation and resolutely choose the right, when there are strong motives arrayed on the opposite side; who can say with the ancient patriarch, "Till I die, I will not remove my integrity from me." But the spontaneous activity of conscience, where there is no distinct exercise of moral choice, takes place under the operation of a Divine law analogous to the all-embracing laws of the material universe. The vast amount of practical goodness that coexists with non-religion, irreligion, and specific forms of vice, should be regarded in the same light in which we view the order and harmony of nature, not with praise to the creature, but with adoration to the Creator, Sustainer, and Preserver. It is the mode in which He holds the race together, that successive generations may have the opportunity of moral choice, that the reign of true virtue may be progressively established, that individual excellence may be multiplied and augmented from age to age, and that in the yet distant era of universal righteousness the earth may be inhabited by those who shall do right, with the free purpose and full energy of mind, heart, and soul.

As regards the subject now in hand, conscience, in its

rectitude, purity, and holiness, is our witness of the rectitude, purity, and holiness of Him who thus maintains his presence with our race, and builds the shrine of his indwelling in every soul of man.

II. The Divine holiness is, secondly, manifested in the structure and the course of the outward universe, so far as they favor and execute the laws of right which conscience recognizes. It was said by the Psalmist, "The saints *shall* inherit the earth," and he need not have used the future; the saints *do* inherit it, reap its revenue, enjoy its benefits. Leaving the life to come out of the account, the good man, however contracted his nominal possessions may be, makes more and gets more out of this world than any amplitude of wealth or loftiness of station can give the bad man. From the minimum of outward means of enjoyment he extracts the maximum of enjoyment.

All vice, all sin, is suicidal. Sensuality in every form detracts even from the sum of merely physical gratification. At the outset of a course of sensual indulgence the pleasure is intense; but at a very early period the capacity of enjoyment wanes, and then utterly ceases, while the morbid craving grows, even under the consciousness of added misery, with every new gratification. I have repeatedly interrogated the self-consciousness of intemperate persons, reformed and unreformed, and I feel warranted in saying that all enjoyment from strong drink ceases before the stage of habitual drunkenness is reached, and that thenceforth, between the craving and the satisfying of the tyrant appetite there is hardly a difference in the degree, but only an alternation in the form of suffering. Human cruelty never invented torture to be compared with that which the sensualist incurs. His body becomes the soul's dungeon, — its walls constantly thickening and closing up so as to shut all the wonted entrances of joy. His senses, deadened on the side of pleasure, no longer avenues of beauty or harmony, or even of gratifying perfumes or flavors, are left still open inlets of pain.

Equally fatal are all social vices to individual happiness. Fraud reacts on the deceiver. Avarice impoverishes the life faster than it increases the wealth. The resentful and malevolent passions can harm no one so much as him who harbors them. On the other hand, every generous affection and noble act enlarges the domain of being, enriches and gladdens the soul, and seldom fails to render the outward condition more ample as to the means of happiness.

In like manner, reverence and devotion, loyalty to the Divine will, the religious consecration of the life, in fine, all the traits and habits that belong to personal piety, are adapted to promote prosperity, honor, domestic peace, social consideration, and the enjoyment of the whole outward world; while he who neglects or scorns his duty to God forfeits unnumbered consolations, blessings, and hopes, and incurs positive and unmixed suffering from experiences which to the religious man are means of inward growth and fountains of a purer joy than he knew before.

The dependence of happiness on character is fully verified in every lengthened life. Could you convene a senate of old men of every style of character, from the hoary profligate to the aged saint, and could each be compelled to declare the convictions which had been forced upon him by his life-experience, there would not be a shade of discrepancy in their testimony as to the dependence of what they had enjoyed or suffered on what they had been; while their utterances would run through the whole diatonic scale, from the wailing minor key of the soul loathing the past and dreading the future, unfit to live and afraid to die, to the jubilant swan-note of him who looks back on a consecrated life, and reaches for the crown and palm and harp of his transfiguration. The proverbs of all nations, which are the condensed experience of mankind, are full of this truth. Earthly and earth-limited, — mere prudential maxims as they seem, — they almost all recognize the identity of happiness with right living, and urge motives of expediency in behalf of the very same virtues to which revelation annexes the hope full of immortality.

Now if the world and the inevitable course of human life are so adjusted by the Supreme Providence as thus to favor goodness and to make the way of transgressors hard, it must needs be that He who created the world and who orders human affairs is himself the impersonation of the law embodied in his works and their administration, — the law of truth, purity, and love. Thus the holiness of God, affirmed by revelation, is verified equally by the human conscience and by the whole economy of nature and of life.

Christianity not only declares the Divine goodness and holiness, which are verified, as we have seen, by the religion of nature. It has for its central personage a being who professes to be more than a revealer of truth, — who claims to be received as standing in a peculiar relation to God and to humanity, as the Mediator between God and man, as the representative of the Divine person, as a faultless model for the imitation of the race. Let us see what natural religion says to these claims.

1. Is the mediatorial office which the Scriptures attribute to Jesus Christ intrinsically probable? Here we encounter the prevalent naturalism of our time, which asks, proudly

and scornfully, "Why should I go to God through a mediator, and not rather avail myself of a child's right to look directly into the Father's face, and cast myself, without pledge, promise, or intervention, upon his love?" By parity of reason we might say, "Why, when I want to feast my eyes on the varied landscape, the ocean, the distant hills, should I permit these intrusive sunbeams to gleam over the fields, play on the hillsides, and flash from the waves? Let me rather go abroad in the moonless and starless night, when there is nothing to intervene between my vision and the objects it would rest upon." Nothing, indeed, except dimness and distance. And there has never been anything but dimness and distance to obstruct the clear view of the Divine Being for the nations and the men that have not looked to him through Christ. From the very necessity of the case, the Divine presence, power, and love diffused through the universe cannot be converged on the mental retina of a new-born, limited, earth-bound mortal. A form in which those rays that stream from and over all nature are converged and made visible, in which love is pledged, pardon proffered, protection guaranteed, the Father's arms folded about his children, is an imperative demand of natural religion. For souls born of God must yearn to know him. Souls conscious of sin must crave forgiveness and reconciliation. Souls needy and dependent must long for express assurance, sensible manifestation of the Supreme Providence. This demand was urged by the greatest and wisest minds of Pagan antiquity, and was the subject of their undoubting foresight no less than of Hebrew prophecy. In this sense Jesus the Mediator was the desire of all nations.

2. This manifestation of God needed to be made in human form, and natural religion would anticipate the

manifestation in this form. We can conceive in God of no attributes of which we have not the capacity in ourselves. He may have other attributes; but if so, we cannot attain to the knowledge of them in this life, and can learn them in heaven only by the development of new powers in our own natures. As I have shown you in the earlier part of this course, miracles are adequate to reveal the Divine personality. God becomes known as a person by visibly detaching himself from his works and from the order of nature; by presenting himself as a will and a power supreme over the impersonal forces of the universe; by those acts of sovereignty in which, in the sublime language of Scripture, "He bowed the heavens and came down," — in which his voice was heard and his arm beheld by the astonished nations. Thus far the Hebrews — and they alone of all the ancients — had just conceptions of the Supreme Being. But their idea of God was imperfect, simply because it had not been derived from a perfect incarnation, — because perfect humanity had not been seen. Their God was the Sovereign, but not the Universal Father. He was angry, and needed to be appeased by sacrifice. He was their friend, but not the friend of the whole race of man. He partook of the narrowness and the unlovely passions of a bigoted, jealous, morose, and vindictive people. The imprecatory Psalms, while they represent the darker aspects of the characters of the best men among the posterity of Jacob, as truly represent the limitations of their knowledge of the Supreme Being, as the Psalms of lofty trust and praise exhibit, along with the profound and earnest piety of the writers, their just conceptions of all of the Divine nature that could be revealed without being incarnated.

But in Jesus we behold all contrasts of goodness combined and harmonized, — the strong and the tender, the Judge and the Father, holiness and gentleness, freedom from sin and sympathy with the sinner, — the traits which by themselves would constrain profound and awe-stricken reverence, and those which by themselves would draw out the intimacy and warmth of fraternal affection. In him righteousness and mercy, justice and love, are made one. We see in him not merely the massive elements of character, but equally the delicate tracery of sentiment, the perfectness of spiritual beauty, — all that can bring him near to the common scenes of life, all that we gladly associate with an omnipresent witness and an unfailing friend. When through him as a medium of vision we look to God, while the Divine grandeur and glory are presented up to and beyond our power of conception, we at the same time learn to attach to the Author of our being all that is lovely and beautiful in a perfect human being, all of humanity except its follies and its sins, all in which God's noblest creation can have been the embodied thought of the Creator.

In point of fact, the largest, loftiest, most self-justifying conception of the Deity that has ever been attained by man is the Christian conception; and this extends just so far as the individual thinker can take in the character of Christ, and no farther. Thus, were Christ now on earth, we could go to him for pardon, counsel, and help, without question or misgiving, as we would go to a father, were he no less able than willing to meet all our needs; and just so far as Christ awakens in us this sentiment of familiar trust, do we discern in his person, as we can through no other medium, how the Eternal Father clasps around the needy, the suffering, and the sinning the embrace of ineffable tenderness, — how for every want, in weariness and in grief, under the burden of one's own heart, in the intense agony of self-reproach, man's true recourse is to the bosom of everlasting love.

Now the argument which I would urge is this. The views of the Divine character of which I have spoken, those which connect with God's infinite power, wisdom, and majesty an equal perfectness in the tender, genial, amiable aspects of character, are exclusively Christian in their source. Even revelation does not give them, — they come from manifestation alone, from a theophany. If I may use the words in a sense in which they correspond not to a limiting dogma, but to universal Christian consciousness, they come from " God manifest in the flesh." But thus derived, they are, as I have said, self-justifying. Once suggested, they form the only conception of God which we can thenceforth deem tenable. They commend themselves as intrinsically probable. They are confirmed by our growing knowledge of nature. They are verified equally by our external experience, and by their benign efficacy in moulding our characters and governing our lives. Received from Christ, they become to us in the profoundest and most intimate sense natural, so that, were we forced to surrender them, nature would lose its identity, and become unnatural. From all this the legitimate conclusion is, that the manifestation, the theophany, which thus shows us what God is, is itself natural, and was to have been anticipated. So far is it from standing in the contrast to natural religion in which even Christians have been wont to place it, that the religion of nature would be incomplete without it.

3. I would next speak of Christ as the model for human virtue. The identity of Christianity with natural

religion is seen in the unchanged and unchangeable beauty, lustre, and glory of its Founder's character. He is the only luminary in the moral universe which has no secular parallax, — which appears the same from century to century, the same by the refined and exalted standard of modern times that he did by the rude and gross standard of his own day. While he was upon earth, in a corrupt age and among a degenerate nation, it might seem no wonder that he moved like a very god among men. That the multitude strewed their garments on his path; that the officials of the High-Priest, when sent to arrest him, could not find it in their hearts to lay hands on him; that the centurion who went to keep guard, as at the execution of a malefactor beneath contempt, exclaimed, "Surely this man was a son of God," — these might have seemed the not unnatural testimonials of spontaneous reverence to the power of superior excellence at a period when virtue was rare, and moral heroism was seldom, in its passive forms never, witnessed. But as from that low stand-point we ascend to the higher planes of human goodness, we find the admiration for him undiminished. None so revere him as they who are themselves the most worthy of reverence. None feel so humbled in comparison with him, as those who only gain lustre by comparison with the best beside him.

May I not appeal to individual experience for the result of prolonged familiarity with his character? Other historical personages we can study to excess, — we become weary of them, and they are belittled to our apprehension. We can take in all that they were and all that they accomplished, — we can go round them and over them, and the greatest of them constitutes so small a portion of the world's greatness, and shapes so small a portion of the world's history, that he becomes dwarfed in the very attempt to compass and comprehend his magnitude. The fame of some popular hero is often thus injuriously affected by our having read and heard too much about him, though it be all to his praise. But who gets tired of Christ, or feels that he has exhausted His fulness? He occupies the lowest place with those who know him least. He grows upon our study. New lines and hues of spiritual beauty reveal themselves with every fresh perusal of the evangelic record; there is new meaning in his acts, new force in his words. On intimate conversance with his life, indifference passes into respect, respect deepens into reverence, reverence glows into adoration. More and more does the human become divine, as we behold the glory of God in the face of Jesus Christ. None look so lovingly into his countenance as those whose wonted place is with John on the bosom of their Lord. We can conceive of no change in the picture which would not be for the worse. There is no defect, no excess, no redundancy.

But if in the moral character of Jesus there is nothing that belongs peculiarly to his age or nation, nothing conventional, nothing transient or capable of being outgrown, in fine, if it is wholly unaffected by the time and space element, then that character must be, not by hyperbole, but literally, divine, — and if divine, then natural, — derived from and conformed to that nature which is absolute, unchangeable goodness and holiness. In revering and following Christ, we are rendering honor to God and imitating him, and the religion which consists in this is pre-eminently natural; for what can be so natural as for the creature to honor the Creator, — for the intelligent and self-determining creature to imitate Him from whom he derived the power of thought, will, and choice? In the light in which I have now presented Christ as an exemplar of human goodness, (though I by no means deny the more strictly dogmatic sense commonly attached to such phraseology,) Christ was before Abraham, before the worlds; he manifested that which was truth and right in the beginning, absolute goodness, eternal rectitude; and the religion based on his life belongs to the organism of the spiritual universe, and is therefore, in the strictest and most intimate sense, the religion of nature.

As the Mediator, as the image of God, as the model of perfect humanity, we have thus seen that Christ, standing though he does alone in history, heralded by prophecy, authenticated by miracle, is still a natural personage,— a being whose advent might have been anticipated on grounds connected with the nature of God and of man. We may, I think, go still further, and inquire, without irreverence, under what outward circumstances it was antecedently probable that such a manifestation would be made.

1. We might, in the first place, expect that the birth and parentage of this personage would be exempted from all intrinsically or reputedly mean and vulgar associations, — from all that would of necessity make him the object of contempt and scorn. How far was this condition fulfilled in Jesus? His reputed parents, though poor, were not paupers. Though they were in humble condition, all the notices we have of them authorize the assertion that they and their kindred and associates were respectable and respected, industrious, intelligent, and virtuous, bearing no brand that would exclude them from favored recognition in so democratic a state of society as then pre-

vailed in Judæa. The legal necessity of their going from Nazareth to Bethlehem for registration shows that they were not mere proletaries, but that they were possessed of some slender freehold in the latter of these cities, while the tradition runs that they owned a house in the former. Their descent from the ancient royal line, though so remote, and shared by so many, as to create no aristocratic prestige, yet enhanced their self-respect, and gave them a certain degree of social consideration.

2. In the next place, it was equally fitting that the being who was to stand in this official relation between God and man should have none of the ordinary claims to distinction and eminence. Wealth, rank, place, or title, so far as it had any prominence in his condition, would tend to diminish the lustre of his character. Heaven's purest gems need no setting, and shine brightest when they shine alone. He who is to draw all men to himself by the beauty and majesty of his spirit, should have nothing in his surroundings which will bring to him a spurious homage, an interested clientship, adherents to his earthly fortunes and not to his supra-mundane sovereignty. Even Jesus, in his want and careful abnegation of all that ordinarily draws parasites, was at one time harassed by men who sought him because they had been fed by him in the desert. How constantly and annoyingly would this experience have been repeated, had he had a mansion and a table of his own! The scanty funds contributed for his wayfaring by grateful disciples tempted the cupidity of one bad man, and that one was the most important and serviceable member of the apostolic college; for his testimony is of priceless worth. Could he have charged his Master with the shadow of wrong, he might have made his thirty pieces of silver thirty thousand, and his employ-

ers, if they had not had money enough, would have levied contributions throughout Judæa for the deficit; but when he turned traitor, there was absolutely nothing for him to betray except the spot where the homeless Saviour was going to pass the night. But had there been that in Christ's outward condition which could be preyed upon, his public appearance at a time when the expectations of his people were so intensely raised, would have attracted a horde of such miscreants. Then, too, any definite rank which could be looked up to by the multitude would have removed him from the sympathy of those beneath him, while he would have stood on an arena, on which even faultless excellence could not have exempted him from paltry rivalries and jealousies. It was necessary that in his worldly estate he should be at once above contempt and beneath envy.

3. Above all, it was necessary that he who should bear the Divine image, and stand forth as the world's exemplar, should be "a man of sorrows, and acquainted with grief"; that he should tread the darkest passages of the earthly pilgrimage, and the valley of the death-shadow. It is the tendency of human thought to connect all painful experiences — penury, suffering, and death — with the Divine displeasure, to regard afflictions as judgments of Heaven, and even to brand the victims of signally heavy calamities as sinners beyond all others. How numerous are the traces of this habit of mind in the sacred writings! It forms, as you know, the burden of the harangues of several among the interlocutors in the dramatic poem of Job; it is referred to repeatedly in the Psalms, and was on several occasions forced on the animadversion of Christ. At the same time, we find it not infrequently recognized in the ancient classics. Only through the

destitution, homelessness, agony, and cross of the Sinless One did the world learn that him whom God loves He chastens. Then, too, it is in these experiences that man most needs both example and sympathy, — the example of submission, trust, and hope, the sympathy of one who has endured and overcome. The suffering now look to Christ in his agony, and repeat his prayer, "Not my will, but thine, be done," till pain and grief are merged in resignation, and turned to joy by the hope that is full of immortality. The dying look to the grave as the place where the Lord lay, and whence he rose, and calmly and rejoicingly commit their departing spirits to their Father. Grief is transfigured by his endurance; death is swallowed up in victory by the might of his cross and the power of his resurrection.

The influence of a suffering Redeemer has left its indelible traces in language, which often embodies in single words whole chapters of human history. Before he suffered, the terms that denoted sad experiences were all such as represented only the malignant aspect of what man endured, or, at best, the single fact of endurance. Take, for instance, the word *calamitas* (calamity), the condition, some say, of the *blighted stalk*, which bears no ear of grain; others, of the *broken reed*.[1] To Tertullian,[2] the earliest of the Latin Fathers, belongs, I believe, the appropriation of the first word that tells the whole story, expresses the divine side, the blessed ministry of sorrow, — *tribulatio* (tribulation), — *threshing*, the process by which

---

[1] Wedgwood regards *calamitas* as not improbably derived from the root which furnishes, in the Welsh, *col*, denoting *loss* or *misfortune;* a root which he traces in the Latin *incolumis*, expressing the negation of loss or misfortune. If we admit this derivation, the word *calamitas* is still void of any spiritual or hopeful significance.

[2] *Adversus Judæos*, 11.

the elements of character are separated, the chaff given to the winds, the wheat heaped up for the harvest of which the angels are the reapers.

I have thus shown you that in the person and relations of Christ as Mediator, as the image of God, as the exemplar of man, we have precisely the offices which on *a priori* grounds we should anticipate from the loving providence of God; and that in his condition in life, his sufferings, and his death, we have the very elements which alone could have met the needs of man, and thus have satisfied the postulate of natural religion.

LECTURE IX.

IMMORTALITY.

AMONG the contents of the Christian revelation, next in intrinsic importance to the Divine attributes is the immortality of the soul. In my first Lecture I showed you that in the nature of things immortality cannot be an object of consciousness, or a necessary inference from known premises; that there are in the external universe analogies both for and against it; and that analogy, even could it be urged on the affirmative side alone, proves nothing, but is valid only as an answer to objections against truths or beliefs that rest on independent grounds of argument and evidence. A life beyond death can be made certain only by revelation direct or mediate, verbal or phenomenal, — by the authenticated testimony of a divine messenger, or by the return to this world of those whom we call dead, to teach us that death is a name and not a fact. Yet if man is destined for a higher sphere of being, we should expect to find some birth-marks of this destiny, and some features in his outward condition here and in the structure and course of the visible universe that harmonize with this hypothesis rather than with the theory of annihilation. It is in this direction that I now propose to guide your inquiry.

In the first place, death, so far as we know, is a merely physical change; its observed phenomena are solely material; and if there be an immaterial principle in man, a soul that depends not on the bodily organism for its existence and its capacity of perception, thought, and emotion, it is at least possible that the soul may live on when the body dies. What evidence then have we of the immateriality of the soul? Consciousness, it is commonly maintained, affirms the soul to be immaterial. The self-conscious ME does not identify itself with the limbs and the organs. We habitually think of them as not themselves perceiving, reflecting, judging, but as instruments which *we* employ for these ends, — as not themselves powers, but as the irresponsible agents of a controlling power, — as belonging philosophically to the same category with lenses, canes, and calculating-machines. When we use the word *I*, we mean by it something more than the whole body, — something which imparts to the multiform body a oneness other than that which belongs to it by virtue of its mere structure (which latter oneness, we know, is literally dissolved in death), — something which owns the body as its property, and commands it as its servant.

> "The purple stream which through my vessels glides
> Dull and unconscious flows, like common tides.
> The pipes through which the circling juices play
> Are not that thinking I no more than they.
> This frame, compacted with transcendent skill
> Of moving joints obedient to my will,
> Nursed from the fruitful glebe, like yonder tree,
> Waxes and wastes. I call it mine, not me."

If mind is the result of material organization, then every mental action must be a material process and product. If a mere process, we might apply to it a theory corresponding to the undulatory theory of light and heat, and it is at least conceivable that vibrations of the brain, or electric impulses sent along those magnetic wires, the nerves, should cause the modes of being which we designate as ideas, judgments, and emotions. But the permanence of these modes of being is fatal to the undulatory hypothesis. Every mental action is not only a process, but a product. Something is inwrought which remains in existence. Permanent modifications of the consciousness are made during every waking hour. In order to render memory possible on the materialistic hypothesis, every throb of a nerve, every vibration of the brain, must leave its life-long traces in the material structure. But to conceive of this carries us immeasurably beyond the marvellous disclosures of microscopic discovery. Myriads of legible and enduring entries must be made within every needle's point of the brain. If the unnumbered words, dates, facts, and experiences that lie in the memory make each some permanent notch, furrow, or mark, of whatever kind, or however minute, the brain in very infancy would be too full to admit of added mental growth. Physically, it is as utterly impossible for a life-record to be kept within the walls of a human cranium, as it would be for a year's accounts of the United States Treasury to be transcribed on half a sheet of note-paper.

It may, indeed, be objected to this reasoning, that in point of fact mental action depends for its precision, vigor, and brilliancy on the degree in which the bodily organization is symmetrical and healthful, and especially on the shape and size of the cranium. I answer, that this would of necessity be the case, equally on the materialistic and on the immaterial hypothesis. The question is not as to the means, but as to the seat and source, of mental action. The immaterialist by no means denies the instrumentality of the bodily organization, — its necessary instrumentality during the present state of being. The body is the soul's case of tools, and the quality of the soul's action must depend on the strength and temper of those tools. Unless they are in good order, the soul must work, either not at all, as in idiocy, or languidly, as in imbecility, or without reasonable purpose, as in insanity. But this liability to inferior execution here by no means proves that the soul is incapable of surviving its present set of tools, and, with better instruments, of doing ample justice to a skill and power native, but unsuspected now. Give the most accomplished artist dull or clumsy instruments, his work will be vastly below a master's hand; but his taste and genius, though hidden from human eye, remain unimpaired, nor will his present rough and ill-shapen productions prevent him from one day rivalling Canova, should he be surrounded with the material aids through which alone Canova could give form to his conceptions. This temporary dependence, yet essential and ultimate non-dependence, of the soul on the body is well illustrated in these stanzas from Sir John Davies's poem on the Immortality of the Soul: —

> "As a good harper, stricken far in years,
> Into whose cunning hands the gout doth fall,
> All his old crotchets in his brain he bears,
> But on his harp plays ill, or not at all; —
>
> "But if Apollo takes his gout away,
> That he his nimble fingers may apply,
> Apollo's self will envy at his play,
> And all the world applaud his minstrelsy." [1]

There is, then, no conclusive objection to the soul's immateriality derived from the correlation between a well or ill developed brain and a well or ill working mind; while the affirmative argument from consciousness and

[1] *Original, Nature, and Immortality of the Soul,* Section xxxiii.

memory remains unimpeached. But if the soul be immaterial, it is a separate existence from the body, and the disorganization of the body cannot destroy it. If it dies with the body, it must nevertheless die by a direct act of annihilation, or by the reabsorption into the universal soul affirmed by pantheism, which is simply a euphemism for annihilation. But annihilation has never occurred within human experience or observation. The death of organized being is only a separation of particles, which enter forthwith into new combinations, and generally into new forms of life. The very phenomena of death, therefore, as they involve no destruction of any visible or tangible portion of the being that dies, furnish a strong presumptive argument against the destruction by death of the immaterial portion of the being, of which the senses cannot take cognizance.

But if the soul survive the body, how can it live on in self-consciousness and activity? How, without a bodily organization, can it retain its conversance with the physical universe? How can sights reach the soul without the eye, or sounds without the ear? How can locomotion take place without material organs, to overcome material resistance? I reply, that, in point of fact, the ideas of things seen, heard, and felt reach the consciousness, not only without the aid of the organs of sense, but without the existence of corresponding objects in the outward universe. In insanity, sights which the eye sees not, sounds which the ear hears not, are inwardly perceived with the utmost vividness. In dreams, too, we seem to see, hear, and feel as distinctly as when the senses are all awake, and conversant with their appropriate objects. Now if the soul can receive these several classes of impressions without employing the organs of sense, why may it not without possessing them? Or if it be capable of seeing, hearing, and feeling things that are not, how can we affirm that it is incapable of perceiving things that are? Moreover, it is not the eye that sees, or the ear that hears.[1] Dissect these organs entire from the human frame, they are powerless. Leave them entire, and darken the soul by insanity, they carry it false reports. It is the soul that looks out through the eyes and listens through the ears. And does not its power of seeing and hearing by means of these instruments imply and include a perceptive power which might be exercised through other instrumentalities, or directly and without medium? It is at least a tenable hypothesis, that sight and hearing, and locomotion also, are functions inherent in the soul; and that the bodily organization is less the means of their exercise, than a temporary limit and hinderance to their extent and power. It may be that we in our present state are spirits in prison, — that the eye is the prison-window through which the soul enjoys a little portion of its native range of vision, the ear an aperture in the prison-wall through which we catch a few of the sounds which, if set at large, we might take in through a vast extent of space, while the feet, so far from being the means of motion, only measure the direction and length of the spirit's chain. If this be true, when the dungeon-walls decay, when we quit our house of bondage, our disembodied souls may acquire at once a keenness of vision of which we cannot now conceive, hear the full diapason of nature's harmony, and move

[1] "Nos enim ne nunc quidem oculis cernimus ea, quæ videmus; neque enim est ullus sensus in corpore, sed, ut non solum physici docent, verum etiam medici, qui ista aperta et patefacta viderunt, viæ quasi quædam sunt ad oculos, ad aures, ad nares, a sede animi perforatæ." — Cicero, Tusc. Quæst. I. 20.

unchecked and free at every prompting of love or duty.[1]

But this is not the only, nor to my mind the most probable hypothesis. It is entirely conceivable that a virtual resurrection of the body may be coincident with its death; not, indeed, the recombination of the precise material elements that were combined before death (which, if it take place, can be realized only at some far-off resurrection epoch), but the re-embodiment of the soul in an organism allied to and developed from that which has here been its dwelling-place, so that it shall be, in apostolic language, "not unclothed, but clothed upon." Some-

---

[1] "Nam nunc quidem, quanquam foramina illa, quæ patent ad animum a corpore, callidissimo artificio natura fabricata est, tamen terrenis concretisque corporibus sunt intersepta quodam modo. Cum autem nihil erit præter animum, nulla res objecta impediet, quo minus percipiat, quale quidque sit." — Tusc. Quæst. I. 20.

This view of the (so-called) organs of sense as avenues rather than instruments of perception, and of the soul as endowed with the power of exercising independently the functions which it exercises through these avenues, is well expressed in these quaint stanzas of Henry More: —

> "Like to a light fast lock'd in lanthorn dark,
> Whereby by night our wary steps we guide
> In shabby streets, and dirty chanels mark ;
> Some weaker rayes from the black top do glide,
> And flusher streams perhaps through th' horny side.
> But when we've past the perill of the way,
> Arrived at home, and laid that case aside,
> The naked light how clearly doth it ray,
> And spread its joyful beames as bright as summer's day!

> "Even so, the soul in this contracted state,
> Confined to these straight instruments of sense,
> More dull and narrowly doth operate ;
> At this hole heares, the sight must ray from thence,
> Here tasts, there smells. But when she 's gone from hence,
> Like naked lamp she is one shining spheare,
> And round about has perfect cognoscence
> What ere in her horizon doth appear;
> She is one orb of sense, all eye, all airy ear."

thing of this kind may be implied in those words of St. Paul, " Thou sowest not that body that shall be, ... but God giveth it a body as it hath pleased him." Matter has all conceivable and inconceivable degrees of tenuity. Science admits the existence, concurrently with the atmosphere through its whole extent, and in the interstellar spaces where there is no atmosphere, of an impalpable and imponderable ether, which transmits the calorific waves of the sunlight and the undulations of the solar, lunar, and stellar rays. Mind must be either infinite and omnipresent, which but one mind can be, or else localized and circumscribed by some organism, which need not be gross or dense, but may have as little of earthiness as this ether in which the planets move, which yet shall give it a place in the creation, and shall enable it to act on and to be acted upon by other beings and objects in the universe. And it is entirely conceivable that by means of some such organism the soul in dying may retain its personality, nay, more, may preserve all that constituted its individual identity, even what might recall wonted associations with form and feature, voice and manner, and render it distinctly recognizable by fellow-spirits.

I suggest these hypotheses, not as solving the mystery which " the great teacher, Death," alone can solve, but to show that, if the soul be immaterial, there is nothing in the dissolution of the body which should render its survivance of that event impossible or improbable.

I would next speak of the presumption in behalf of the survival of the soul after death derived from the changes during life which it survives. Organic life is perpetual decomposition and reconstruction; in other words, constant death and birth. There is probably not a particle of matter in one of our bodies which was there half a dozen years ago; and, death excepted, there can hardly be a more entire physical change than occurs between childhood and manhood, or between twenty and fourscore, the change being not only one of size, shape, strength, and voice, but often of the whole physical constitution, — the puny child that can hardly be kept alive growing into a stalwart youth, the invalid outliving the infirmities of many years and becoming a vigorous old man; or, on the other hand, the fairest promise of health and strength undermined by functional disease, of which there was not a trace visible in the child or the young man. Death differs from these changes, not in its entireness, but only in its suddenness, and the capacity of the soul to retain its identity while the physical frame gradually loses its identity certainly involves the same capacity in the more rapid and paroxysmal loss of the physical identity in death.

Consider, too, the lesion of the bodily organs by sickness or accident, in which the soul retains its integrity. Not only may the limbs be amputated, the eyes quenched, the lungs almost consumed, but the nerves may be paralyzed, the brain wounded or diseased, and yet the mind may remain unimpaired, the soul unclouded, nay, as if in mockery of mere physical hinderances, the spirit may wield a mightier power and wing a loftier flight than ever before. And in cerebral disease attended by delirium, there is no defect in the quantity and intensity of mental action, but often a preternatural brilliancy and power, though the consciousness ceases to take accurate cognizance of surrounding persons and objects.

Most prophetic of immortality beyond all else in human experience are the phenomena often witnessed up to the very moment of dissolution. I have repeatedly stood by the death-bed of one attenuated by long infirmity, every vital process clogged, the pulse intermittent, the blood already becoming stagnant; and I have seen the dying still in the full vigor of his intellect, master of his position, clearer and stronger in thought and judgment than any one of the by-standers, addressing appropriate counsel or consolation to each of the afflicted circle, dictating messages of love to the absent, and leaving no person or interest forgotten that had the remotest right to a place in his remembrance. I have heard, too, in the hour and in the embrace of death, not the feverish ecstasies of unreasoning fanaticism, but the serene utterances of a mature religious wisdom, of undoubting faith, of quiet trust, of a foreseeing hope that had already crossed the separating stream, and passed within the golden gates; and in the eye kindled with a purer, holier light than ever glows except in the Christian's ascension-room, in the wan countenance radiant with the foreshining of the heavenly day, in the air of joyous expectancy with which the parting moment is waited for and welcomed, the soul's voice is: "Death, I am not thine, and I defy thy power. I am mightier than thou art. Thou art but the doorkeeper of my house not made with hands, my usher into the blessed society of the unfallen and the redeemed." From such a death-scene into annihilation how vast the leap! between them how immeasurable the contrast! while there seems not a step, not even a filmy cloud or an unparted veil, between the scene and heaven. From such a presence unbelief is banished. The sceptical bystander ceases to doubt, always for the moment, often forever; while to the Christian the hand that lifted the widow's son from the bier becomes visible, the voice that called Lazarus from the tomb pulses upon the inward ear in tones that remain unforgotten till he hears them again in his own dying hour.

From these phenomena of approaching death the argument is obvious and strong. Did the soul die with the body, we should certainly expect that it would betray along with the body symptoms of impending dissolution, that its light would be dimmed and flickering, its consciousness confused, its power of consecutive thought impeded, its memory clouded, its hold on wonted beliefs relaxed. But if at that last hour it manifests all and more than all of vitality that was ever witnessed in the prime and joy of its earthly being, there is a strong presumption that it is destined to survive the death-change, and to put off its worn-out garment for its ascension-robe.

I now ask your attention to the arguments for immortality derived from the intellectual and moral nature of man. And first, though, as I showed you in a former Lecture, we cannot be conscious of immortality, we are conscious of an innate and indestructible desire for continued existence. This desire belongs, with rare exceptions, to all developed natures. It is something more than the mere love of the earthly life, for it is often the strongest where that love is the weakest. None have felt it more than those who have offered themselves to death for their country, their race, or their religion. It is a feeling allied to all noble impulses and generous deeds. It has been the fountain-head of all patriotism and philanthropy. It inspires the longing for posthumous fame. It prompts the appeal which the great and good, who have been scorned and vilified by their contemporaries, have so often made to the righteous verdict of posterity, as if they should see themselves justified after their bodies had ceased to be.

Now, if man wholly dies when the body dies, we can hardly reconcile this sentiment, so almost universal in civilized and cultivated communities, with the Divine veracity and integrity.

Another argument for immortality may be drawn from the unsuitableness of the present state of things to man's mental faculties, his capacities of enjoyment, and his conceptions of happiness and perfection. Suppose that you saw an egg for the first time, not knowing what it was, and that you discovered and opened it just as the infant bird was ready to force his way out of the shell. You would see a system of members and organs for which the creature could have no use in that confined condition, — wings and feet without space to fly or walk, a digestive apparatus without the opportunity of procuring food, eyes without a field of vision, in fine, a constitution entirely unsuitable to its present state. Your inference would be, that, though the egg-shell was the creature's birthplace, it was not destined to be its home, — that it was designed for a mode of life in which its organs and faculties could all find their appropriate sphere and exercise their appropriate functions, — that it was created for the light and the air, though now shut out from both.

Man's condition in this world is not unaptly typified by the bird in the shell. He has wings which he cannot here unfold, and eyes of the spirit which find no adequate field of vision here. He has faculties, capacities, and desires, which here seek in vain for free scope and full gratification. He has powers which here are almost dormant, like the cramped pinions of the yet imprisoned bird. He finds the elements of the material universe often hostile, always unsatisfying. He has hardly learned to adapt himself to the world in which he is born, indeed is less adapted to it than the new-born bee or beaver, when he is summoned to leave it. He lives and dies a stranger and a pilgrim here, oftener in conflict than in harmony with his surroundings, oftener yearning for a loftier than contented with a lower sphere. Our intellectual powers grasp at infinity. We are conscious of a boundless capacity of research, knowledge, and progress, and our curiosity grows faster than its gratification, our sense of ignorance faster than our knowledge. In no department of life do we ever reach our aims or embody our conceptions. The painter enshrines in canvas, the sculptor hews from the marble, forms glowing with beauty, redolent of purity and loveliness, vividly lifelike to every beholder; but he has floating before his mind visions of artistical perfectness to which he has hardly begun to give expression. The poet, whose inspiration thrills the universal heart, is tortured by unutterable imaginings, glimpses of glory from the parted heavens, which language cannot clothe, aspirations too lofty and ardent to flow in the broken harmony of earthly song. The man of science who transcends his fellows in his sweeping generalizations is still unsatisfied; for he conceives of profounder depths, more perfect adaptations, broader harmonies, more comprehensive laws, than he has the means of verifying, and each new discovery that dawns on his own mind or is suggested by kindred spirits only fills him with the more earnest desire to bathe forever in exhaustless truth. The pursuit of happiness, too, is pursuit, but less and less attainment. Its fountains are summer-dried or winter-frozen. In the midst of all that can feast the senses or minister to the pride of life, there is still the inward craving for a higher, purer joy. So is it, also, with the noblest of aims, that of moral excellence. However exemplary the character may be, it falls short of its ideal. The good man's goal recedes, his standard grows higher. His endeavors reach out far beyond his attainments, — the spirit willing, but the flesh weak. This disproportion between man and his condition, this constant outreaching, upreaching, is certainly no faint indication of a future state, where our conceptions will be realized and our aspirations satisfied, where our endeavors will overtake our aims, and fruition will answer to desire. It is intrinsically improbable that He, who must love all that is noble in man far more than man can love it, should have implanted these tendencies in our being without providing for their ultimate consummation.

This argument is strengthened when we consider our relations to the visible universe. We are placed within sight of numberless worlds, and are endowed with the capacity of learning something of their relations and laws, but are left in invincible ignorance and intense curiosity as to all else concerning them. Can it be that a good God has opened this gorgeous immensity of creation to our view, to close it forever to our knowledge? Had He destined us to an eternal slumber in the grave, I cannot but think that He would have enveloped us in a denser atmosphere, and not have shown us other worlds than our own.

We might also infer a continuance of life beyond death from the continued growth of the character in extreme old age. The moral principles and habits become more and more profoundly fixed with every added year of a long life, and never appear more characteristically or manifest themselves in fuller vigor than in its last days and scenes. All those powers which are related to the present state alone are liable to decline. The perceptive, apprehensive, and active organs and faculties lose their quickness and keenness. There remains the wonted capacity neither for business nor for enjoyment. Yet there may still be increase of virtue, a progressive refinement and exaltation of character, nay, often a peculiar ripeness and mellowness, as of fruit which grows luscious only as it drinks in the sunbeams through the thinned leafage of autumn. Above all, love, which, the Christian writers tell us, is to outlast faith and hope, to constitute the essence of the heavenly life, to supersede by its loyal affinities and infallible instincts the doubtful reasoning and lame philosophy of this world, so that knowledge in its wonted forms shall cease, to be its own interpreter from spirit to spirit, so that tongues shall fail, — love, both Godward and manward, grows under the lengthening shadows, and is never so radiant and genial as in the latter days of a devout and kind pilgrimage. I knew of an old man of a hundred and five years, blind and deaf, roused only with the utmost difficulty to take notice of the presence of persons and objects around him, whose lips were incessantly moving during his waking hours in audible and fervent praise and prayer; and I could number up (and so could some of you, I doubt not) a goodly list of old men and women who have seemed to belong more to the heavenly society than to the world in which they lingered, and with whom our converse has been like that of Bunyan's Pilgrim with the Shining Ones who walked at times in the country of Beulah, on the hither side of the death-river. In our domestic and social circles have we not a like experience in the tender sympathy, the persistent charity, the forbearing, forgiving, exhaustless affection, the intense kindliness of our aged kindred and friends, who never seem so dear as when they are spared beyond the wonted term of the earthly life? Now this growth of that which constitutes all moral, spiritual vitality, after the law of decrease has superseded that of increase in everything else, this culminating as one declines, this nearing the meridian of a higher sphere as one approaches the earthly horizon, indicates, as seems to me, with clear and strong emphasis, the survivance of the moral nature when dust returns to dust.

A like inference may be obviously drawn from the strength of our specific attachments to individuals. Is it conceivable that God would have made natural affection so intense and tender, — would have bound heart with heart by such close-clinging filaments of common feeling, — had he not intended that friendship and love should be deathless?

A strong argument for immortality is derived from the waste which we must suppose in God's spiritual universe, if there be no higher life. You know how very large a proportion of our race die in early infancy, and how many more die before they have reached a maturity adequate to any of the trusts or duties of active life. Nor do I believe that it is a mere fancy that is implied in the classic saying, "Whom the gods love die young." The very delicacy of organization which attends and cherishes the richest developments of mind and heart, and the cerebral fulness and activity which are often the accompaniments and tokens of the most beautiful promise, with sad frequency are morbid indications, and give presage of early death. This is strange and inexplicable, if death be what it seems. We cannot reconcile with God's perfect wisdom or with his unchanging goodness this wanton destruction of so large a part of the beauty and loveliness, the hope and joy, of our race. But the mystery ceases when we take the higher life into our view. It is natural that the fruit first ripe should be first gathered, — natural that the most hopeful subjects of nurture and instruction should be placed under conditions pre-eminently favorable to their growth, — natural that some at least of the most delicate and sensitive spirits should be spared the rude vicissitudes and stern conflicts through which alone their earthly path to heaven could lie.

A still stronger case of waste is presented in the lives, not cut short in infancy, but developed and matured in strength and beauty, yet with no scope for earthly enjoyment, no adequate mode of self-expression or post of service, no experience save of the obscure and shady side, the trial and the bitterness of life. Here, for instance, is a widow, alone and desolate, sustaining her needy age by incessant and exhausting toil. Her sun was darkened in its very morning, her midway walk was under gathering clouds, and they have settled down upon her declining years in a density which death alone can dissipate. In every relation she has been bereaved, in every earthly prospect disappointed. She has indeed in her spirit been strengthened and exalted, and the flow of her thoughts is serene and heavenly. She loves her Saviour, and his love is the light of her darkness, the joy of her desolation. But with a character richly trained by this arduous discipline, her influence is but little felt in a very contracted circle. Spiritually capable of large usefulness, she has neither the conventional culture, the position, the leisure, nor the means for doing aught for the service of God and man beyond the beautiful example of her patient waiting and submissive trust. She has been educated worthily of an extended and lofty sphere of duty; she has but the narrowest and humblest. Yet God reigns. Is it possible that her training is to no purpose? that she has been made a sport for calamity with no ulterior prospect of a condition worthy of her capacity and her character? Can the extinction of being await her at death? Do not such instances (and they are by no means rare) point with unerring prophecy to a time when God will make up his jewels, — when gems here unset shall grace the dia lem of the King of kings? Do they not indicate a field of duty for which He is educating his most loyal servants, — a charge adequate to the capacity so painfully brought forth and perfected, — a stewardship over many things for those who have been found thus faithful in few things?

I pass to another argument. The strife among the disciples of Jesus for the chief places about their Master's person when he should enter upon his kingdom is the type of a strife perpetually waged in the world, and which has its source in the native and indestructible instinct of self-advancement. It is one of the tokens of the imperfection of this world, good as it is, and one of the natural and perpetual prophecies of immortality, that there are not great places enough here for all who have the capacity and the desire to fill them, and, still more, that what great places there are, are often not filled by great men, but that there is a pretty general misplacing of people, the small in great places, the great in small places, as if this were a nursery of souls rather than their final home, — the anteroom in which they are waiting to be sorted and ranked, not the palace in which they are to assume their several posts of service. The world has indeed its standard; but that standard is more likely to be shortened to the measure of those below it, than to be stretched to the stature of those above it. Some who are not worthy of the world secure its favor, while those of whom the world is not worthy almost always forfeit its favor. Thus who would have recognized as the first man of his age St. Paul, at the whipping-post, in the stocks, on board the prison-ship, chained to two Roman soldiers, his severed head held up for the mockery of a brutal populace? Yet there live many now who think that they see in him a greater manhood than in any being, the Heaven-born alone excepted, who ever trod the earth. But even this posthumous recognition is rare. Of those who have borne all the marks of greatness, how many must there have been for whom there was neither place in their lifetime, nor niche for their names in the memorial tablet of posterity! Most aptly does the Apostle compare this life, with its rewards, to the Olympic games, in which, however many competitors there might be, only one received the prize. Yet all run. Distinction, — greatness of place, relative if not absolute, — pre-eminence among one's fellows, is the universal ambition. Almost all who are not sluggards or sensualists have this aim, and all other aims resolve themselves into this. Thus the scholar seldom so loves learning for its own sake that he does not covet its reputation also. The artist, with all his love for the beautiful, wants to make for himself a name. The strife of the votaries of fashion is for leadership, for greatness in their own small way. The pursuit of wealth is less for the substance that it may purchase, than for the place that it may give. Yet all these aims are, we know, more likely to fail than to succeed, and unnumbered persons with vast desires and large endeavors are kept in or below mediocrity. The effort, too, is one of rivalry, and therefore has its bad side, its malignant aspect. The aim is to overtop and outdo one another. The strife to be the greatest involves the endeavor to make others less; for there is no high earthly platform on which there is room for more than a few to stand.

But God cannot have made this desire to excel an indestructible element of our nature, without giving us a field for its successful exercise without the passion of emulation or rivalry. It cannot be pre-eminence, but excellence by a positive standard, for which He would have us strive. There must be somewhere an arena in which all can so run that they may obtain. There must be somewhere great places enough for all who seek them. But there are not here. We are constrained, then, to look to the life eternal, where alone there can be as many prizes as there are competitors, as many great places as there are great souls.

The arguments for immortality which I have cited are, I know you will agree with me, strong, weighty, conclusive. They seem independent of revelation. Yet they are all derived from Christian culture, many of them from Christian experience; and they seem the most forceful to those who look primarily to Christ for the hope full of immortality, and then hear his revelation echoed from nature and experience. And, more than all, they come to us most genially in our unburdened and happy hours. We rejoice in them; we are thankful for them. But in our times of need and dread, in our depression and sorrow, in the hour of bereavement and under the shadow of death, our cry is, — "Lord, to whom shall we go? Thou hast the words of eternal life."

LECTURE X.

CHRISTIAN MORALITY.

Two years ago, my colleague, Professor Peirce, who in his own department has no superior among living men, delivered from this platform a course of Lectures, in which he constructed a theoretical universe. He took his stand outside of the visible creation, assumed merely the existence of brute matter and certain fundamental mathematical laws, and determined by a masterly line of *a priori* reasoning what the proportions and relations of a universe constructed in accordance with those laws must have been. The result was the coincidence, point for point, of this universe of theory with the actually existing universe. Now imagine a being who could occupy with regard to the entire realm of spiritual existence the position which our great mathematician holds as to the outward creation, — a being of perfect moral wisdom, — of such clear perceptions of actions, their tendencies, and their issues as might suit our conventional idea of a Gabriel, — and let there be propounded to him this problem: "Given the existence of God and of a race of intelligent moral beings, to construct on these data a moral system, which shall insure and preserve harmony and beneficial relations between God and his creatures, as they are maintained by mathematical laws between God and his worlds." The system which would satisfy the conditions of this problem could be no other than the Gospel of

Christ, not a precept, prohibition, or sanction wanting. Wipe out from the memory of earth and heaven every vestige of Christ's life and teachings, let there be wholly unoccupied ground for a new lawgiver, and let one arise of supreme and comprehensive wisdom, he could do no more than republish the moral system of the New Testament. Who can add to this system? or take from it? What conceivable case of obligation is there which it does not reach and meet? What conceivable case in which departure from it is safe? It is not law for man alone, — it must be law wherever being is. Range in thought from planet to planet, — imagine the forms and aspects of life in them all as various as are the combinations of elements in their physical structure, or the celestial panoramas which make their night-seasons glorious, — still you can imagine no other law. You can conceive of no possible condition in which the Sermon on the Mount would not have the same validity which it has with us. Nor as you look into the depths of eternity can you conceive of a stage or degree of progress, at which that compend of duty shall cease to be sole and sufficient law for angels and just men made perfect.

But from some quarters there comes a counter-statement. Let us meet it. It is said by those who think that they have outgrown Christianity: — "There is nothing cosmopolitan in the Gospel. It is all Hebrew, Jewish, belonging to Christ's own age. He gave, indeed, good advice for his time; but it is only by a pious sham, by a well-meant but palpable fiction, that we apply it to the nineteenth century. In the enhanced complications and responsibilities of these modern times, we virtually recognize many laws of duty that have no counterpart in the New Testament. What, for instance, do we find there of the ethics of commerce, or of international relations? What, that shall be our sufficient and infallible guide in our relations to negro slavery? What, that shall strike the just medium between religious toleration and religious indifference, or between freedom of thought and utterance, and dangerous and reprehensible license? Is not ethical science in its nature progressive? Have we not much clearer and larger views of duty than we find any traces of in the Gospel? Is not this the fact, — that Jesus was the greatest moral teacher of his own age, but that we have outgrown him, and could not afford to go back to him?"

I answer: — By parity of reasoning, the world has outgrown Euclid's Elements of Geometry; for in his day there was only now and then a field to measure, or an altitude to determine, or some very simple geometrical calculation to make, while we are doing a thousand things of which he never dreamed, such as grading railways, constructing massive fortifications, triangulating the seacoast of entire continents. Yet in point of fact Euclid's Elements are the geometry of our time no less than of his. The processes now performed are simply the application of the laws that have come down to us from him to the enlarged and complicated demands of a higher civilization. Without those laws the problems before us would be unmanageable. They are capable of a practical solution only by methods involved in his treatise, and which he would have indicated, had these problems been proposed to him.

In like manner, though there is in the Gospel no statement of the concrete moral problems of the nineteenth century, the only approach we make to their solution is by means of the very principles which Jesus stated in their applications to the problems of his day, and which could have been understood when he promulgated them only through their being thus applied. Indeed, so far are we from having outgrown the Gospel, that we still fall very far short of its scope, and depth, and spirituality. The most that we can say is, that the boasted progress of moral science has been in the direction of Christian morality, — that there has been a growing tendency toward the embodiment of the precepts of the Gospel. In government, in commerce, in political economy, there has been what we term a constant moral progress ever since the Protestant Reformation. Principles at first the subjects of fierce controversy have surmounted opposition, outlived dissent, and come to be regarded as axioms that do not admit of dispute. But when we examine any such axiom, — the vaunted discovery of the present or the last generation, — we always find that it is as old as the Gospel, that it fell perfectly shaped from the lips of Jesus and found explicit record from the pen of the Evangelists, and that its modern form is but a translation of the words of Christ into scientific language, or an application of some broad principle of Christianity to some modern mode of thought or action. In all the departments of concrete ethics, Christianity, so far from being outgrown, is slowly but surely working its way into the hearts of nations, into the great heart of humanity, thus progressively fulfilling the prediction, " Behold, I make all things new."

To verify this view of the Christian morality in all its details, would transcend my present limits; I shall therefore confine my attention to the two prime ethical discoveries or revelations of Christianity, which together cover the whole of human duty, and thus include the very details which I have not time to treat separately.

I. Natural philosophy tells us that the orbits of the heavenly bodies result from the combining of two opposite tendencies; — the centripetal, by which the satellite is attracted to its primary, the planet to the sun, the system to the centre of gravity of the cluster to which it belongs; and the centrifugal, by virtue of which alone the sphere would be hurled on its solitary and darkening path into unknown depths of space, and would be liable to the perilous attraction or ruinous contact of its sister-worlds. The human soul is, by the necessity of its being, subject to these two opposite tendencies; — the centripetal, by which it is drawn to its Source and Author; the centrifugal, by which it is made liable to every form of attraction and influence from its fellow-beings. Accordingly, to the human conscience duty presents itself under these two aspects, — that of supreme devotion to God, and that of paramount obligation to man. Each may be plausibly represented as comprising the whole of duty. It may be urged, on the one hand, that He who has made us all that we are, and has given us all that we have, justly claims all our thoughts, all our powers, all our affections; and that even the charities of life, if they arrest our contemplation of the Infinite One, check the flow of prayer and praise, and interest us in inferior beings and objects, are a robbery of God, a scanting of the incense due on his altar, of the living, perpetual sacrifice by which alone we can be worthy of his love. On the other hand, it may be maintained that we can neither enhance his wealth, nor increase his happiness, nor add to his glory; that the needs and claims of our fellow-men are constant and imperative, demanding all of time and faculty we have; and that the fervor and energy given to devotion are uselessly, wrongfully, and injuriously abstracted from our brethren.

The prime desideratum in a moral system is the just balancing of these centripetal and centrifugal forces, the reconciliation, the unifying, of piety and charity, so that there shall be the maximum of both, and so that each shall render the other more intense and fervent. This is the first moral problem of natural religion, and if Christianity alone solves it, then in this respect Christianity is pre-eminently natural religion. Let us trace these tendencies separately, and then see how they are combined and harmonized in Christianity.

We will first trace the centripetal force unmodified, — the exclusively pietistic theory of duty, of which we have an affluence of examples under both Pagan and Christian auspices. The pietistic impulse may be one of fear. In this case the devotee is haunted by a morbid consciousness of impurity and sin, — *morbid*, I say, for the healthful consciousness of personal delinquency which we cannot feel too profoundly is allayed by penitence, and finds recourse to the fountain of forgiveness opened in the cross of the world's Redeemer. But the devotee's one idea is propitiation by personal sacrifice and suffering, — the buying off of penalty in the world to come by gratuitous torture sought and endured in the present life. Under this impulse, the Hindoo has torn the living flesh from his limbs, hung his quivering frame on hooks of steel, flung himself under the car of Juggernaut, or buried himself in easier suicide under the saving waters of the sacred river. The Christian ascetic, in the same spirit, has abjured all the ties of family and society, fed on street-offal, lived in booths, huts, and caverns in which he could neither stand nor sit, passed years of vigil on pillars, lacerated his body with the hair-cloth and the scourge, courted insult and outrage, gloried in rags, filth, and vermin. Not only have such lives been wasted as regards all valuable human ends. They have been worse than wasted as to the very end of religious culture to which they might seem adapted. The God thus worshipped has been the frightful chimera of a disordered fancy. All imaginable dogmatic atrocities have had their birth in these savage cells and dens. Man learns to conceive worthily of God only through human relations. It is in terms borrowed from these relations that the Scriptures teach the fatherhood of God, and image the soul's espousal to her Redeemer. It is he who lives purely and dutifully in these relations that sees in the human the constantly suggestive symbol of the Divine, and drinks in perpetually a strengthening, gladdening faith in his Father and Saviour. The ascetic, in forfeiting the symbol, loses all sense of what it signifies, and finds his types for the Divinity in the savage scenes, loathsome endurances, and horrible self-tortures, which are his temple, his ritual, and his worship.

Another form of the pietistic impulse is engendered by the action of superstitious belief on indolence and apathy. This has furnished the rank and file of Christian recluses in all ages. The cloisters have been filled for the most part by men and women who might have been stimulated to useful industry by just views of duty, or would have been driven to toil for their subsistence, had not their laziness found sanction and support in a false and harmful charity. The best thing that these religious recluses have been wont to do is to vegetate in an ever nearer approach to idiocy, their faculties gradually rusting away by disuse. Probably from the very prayers and litanies in which their days drag out their weary length, the spiritual element is wholly exhaled at a very early period, and the service of the altar becomes as much a mere bodily exercise as that of the refectory. Where, however, the appetites are strong, they avenge themselves for the violence done to human nature by subduing and dishonoring it. Monasticism has been atrociously wronged whenever it has been represented as the conscious and willing nurse of sensuality. Its discipline has been, for the most part, administered by and upon either honest and fervent ascetics or harmless drones; and I cannot believe, without stronger evidence than the history of the Church gives us, that the intent of evil has at any time mingled largely with the motives that have led men to abjure the living world, which has always offered too many facilities for every form of vice to make a retreat from it tempting to the viciously disposed. Yet even Montalembert, the most eloquent among the eulogists of monastic institutions, admits that foul and horrible excesses of gluttony, drunkenness, and sensuality of every kind, have been not infrequent among the cloistered.* And we should expect this; for idleness and an unoccupied mind always leave free scope and full sway for all the capacity that one has of low appetite and brutal passion. Thus it is that many, who began by sincerely consecrating a profitless life to God, have passed, almost unconsciously, to the opposite camp.

There remains yet another, the mystic type of pietism, of which we cannot speak without profound reverence for the pure and noble spirits which it has given to human-

---

* See Montalembert, *Les Moines d' Occident*, Introduction, Chap. vii. After speaking of the indignant utterances against monastic abuses put by Dante into the mouth of St. Benedict (*Paradiso*, Canto xxii.), and of the coarse and foul portraitures of depravity under the cowl which make up the substance of Boccaccio's *Decamerone*, Montalembert adds: "La corruption monastique devint le lieu commun de la satire, en même temps que la matière constante des doléances trop légitimes de toutes les âmes pieuses comme des plus hautes autorités de l'Église."

ity. Yet even in their case we discern the need of an outward sphere of duty to check the morbid reaction from a too concentrated gaze upon spiritual realities, from a too continuous direct communion with God. There is very apt to grow up in such souls an egotism, modest and humble indeed, yet engrossing and exacting. They become like the hypochondriac invalid, who is perpetually feeling his own pulse. Painful and self-accusing introspection alternates with devotion, and encroaches upon it more and more. Groundless depression blends with the flow of pious thought, and imparts to it a tinge of gloom. The records of such lives leave a sad impression on the reader, and make us feel that, even with the crowning grace of sincere devotion Godward, there is much that contributes to the strength and beauty of character left undeveloped.

The centripetal tendency cannot, then, in any of its exclusive forms, commend itself to our entire approval, even in its religious aspects.

Let us now mark the working of the centrifugal tendency when not balanced by the centripetal, — of social virtue when not inspired and energized by piety. This inquiry is only too timely. It is one of the heresies of our day to estimate the traits and gifts of mind and heart by their immediate mechanical results; and piety, because its direct acts are not earthward and manward, because it does not visibly feed and clothe men, because it does not in its express form go down into the arena of strife and gain, is struck from the list of utilities, its services deemed a waste, its joys a delusion. Yet I maintain that this, and this alone, can give strength, permanence, and purity to the social virtues, — that the life hidden with God is identical with the life that diffuses blessings among men. The fountain is fed from secret springs, and, when it leaps and bubbles fresh and clear, indicates a source higher than its level. The navigable river, the fall that turns the mill-wheel, is made deep and strong by forest-rills that carry no freight, by mountain-torrents too wild and vagrant for industrial uses. Stop the source, the fountain stagnates and dries up. Cut off the rill, the boat is stranded on the river's bed. Arrest the torrent, the wheel stands still. Equally do what are called the useful virtues depend on those which belong to the interior life.

There is in our day a great deal of professed philanthropy where religious faith and reverence are wanting. But did you ever know an undevout philanthropist worthy of the name? These professed friends of their race who neglect the peculiar duties of religion are either partial in their charity, warm in some causes of philanthropy and indifferent or hostile to others; or their zeal is flickering, their torch a revolving, intermittent light; or else they blend with much that is kind and generous a large infusion of bitterness and rancor, so that out of the same mouth proceed blessing and cursing. Without love to God, love to man grows languid. What was heart-work at the outset soon lapses into tongue-work or hand-work; and as tongue or hand for lack of heart grows weary, it either sinks into utter inertness, or, if kept in motion by habit or pressure from without, it pursues its routine peevishly and fretfully, because reluctantly. There is no more pitiable or noxious being than the godless philanthropist. The men who forsake and scorn the altar are the very men who make philanthropy a hissing and a by-word, who cast reproach on the holiest causes, who thwart the sincere benevolence of multitudes that would gladly do all they can for their race, who by their denunciations and anathemas keep back the sober and self-respecting from fields of effort in which they would rejoice to labor.

We have thus seen that of these two tendencies of character neither can be suffered to prevail to the exclusion of the other, without injurious results, nay, more, without failure of the very end pursued, — the mere devotee being dwarfed or distorted in his religious development, the mere philanthropist losing his capacity of usefulness. Yet before Jesus Christ none knew that piety and charity were essential to each other, inseparable allies, neither capable of subsisting apart. Such was the law of nature, and truly good men had lived by this law, yet without knowing it, just as men for several thousand years had experienced the phenomena of the earth's rotation and revolution without any conception of them. Christianity is not peculiar in enjoining piety, or in inculcating charity; for both had formed a part of the better ethical systems of the ancient world. But it was and is peculiar in uniting the two, in affirming the one to be dependent on and inseparable from the other, and in placing that first which is first in the nature and necessity of things, and without which the second cannot be. When Jesus Christ announced as the first and great commandment, "Thou shalt love the Lord thy God with all thy heart," and declared the second, "Thou shalt love thy neighbor as thyself," to be, not separate from it, not independent of it, not the opposite pole of duty, but "like unto it," he proclaimed the most momentous discovery ever made in moral science, — a discovery that bears the same relation to the spiritual world which the discovery of universal gravitation bears to the material universe.

You will remember how this union constitutes the keystone of the New Testament morality, how constantly religious and social duty are united in the teachings of Christ, and how their identity forms the entire burden of that tender, loving epistle of St. John.

But, as Jesus says, the love of God must come first. Without it, there may be a certain amount of good-doing, under the impulse of transient enthusiasm, from the imitative instinct which makes certain modes of beneficence fashionable, or from party spirit, which often confers material relief or comfort in an utterly malignant temper; but there can be no broad, persistent, long-suffering love of man. For of those who most need our love, how many are there who present in themselves nothing on which it can lay hold! Think you that the first missionaries to the Malays, and Hottentots, and New-Zealanders, who attested their love for them by untold sacrifices and sufferings, saw anything to love in those fierce and truculent savages, in those grinning, ape-like negroes, in those cannibals hungering for their flesh, — in those vile kennels and rubbish-heaps of humanity? No. But as we should follow up with our kindest offices a degraded and seemingly worthless brother of a very dear friend, should look on that brother with our friend's eyes, should believe that there was in him worth or the capacity of it because our friend thought so, and should for our friend's sake take a sincere interest in him, so our love to God will reveal to us the precious in man however degraded and imbruted, will make us love him for God's image in him though it be obscured and defaced, and will sustain us in every effort and sacrifice that may help to repair the temple in ruins, and to cleanse the sacred image from its foul and noisome incrustations.

How perfect is the union of these two principles in the

life of Christ, — a life literally in the bosom of the Father, a life consecrated in its entireness to loving offices among the needy, the suffering, the guilty, the abandoned, — the night-watches sequestered from the repose of the toil-worn body for the profounder rest of lonely prayer, the days so crowded with words and works of mercy that some of them of which we can trace the record might seem to have been preternaturally lengthened! Since his time, and in his spirit, all the great workers for humanity have been as fervent in their devotion as they have been energetic in their labor of love. No matter in what department of philanthropic service, — whether it is Howard so engrossed with the prisons that he has no time to look at the palaces and cathedrals of Continental Europe, or Judson coining his whole noble being into labors and sacrifices for benighted Burmah, or Cheverus, with refinement and culture that would have graced a court, building the fire and making the gruel for the sick poor in loathsome Broad-Street cellars, or Charles Wesley pouring forth those sweet redemption-songs whose Sabbath strains echo round the world, or Arnold inaugurating a new era of Christian education, and imparting impulses that will be felt longer than his name will be spoken among men, — wherever there is an energy of love that thrills through all hearts, and commands universal reverence and sympathy, there too is an equal energy of piety. Not a throb of kindly feeling pulses for a fellow-man, that mounts not first to God, and through him descends in blessing. Not a wave of sympathy rolls in upon the stricken heart, that flows not first to the Majesty on high, thence refluent earthward. Not a cord of benign influence is thrown around the degraded and the guilty, that has not its attachment and its purchase on the eternal throne.

II. There is another moral problem, to which I would invite your attention, and which will occupy the remainder of the present Lecture. There is at first view an irreconcilable antagonism between self-love and beneficence. Self-love is inevitable; beneficence is a manifest duty. But if we love ourselves, how can we rob ourselves of time, reputation, ease, or money for the good of others? If we are beneficent, how can we be otherwise than false to that law of our very natures which urges upon us a primary reference to our own happiness? I cannot find that this problem was solved by any moralist before Christ. Beneficence was indeed inculcated before Christ, but as a form of self-renunciation, not as returning a revenue to the kind heart and the generous hand. Yet here Christ plays a bold stroke. His precepts are full of philanthropy. They prescribe the utmost measure of toil and sacrifice for humanity. They constrain the disciple to call nothing his own which others really need, — to hold all that he has subject to perpetual drafts from those who can claim his sympathy. Yet Christ is so far from dishonoring and denouncing self-love, that he cherishes it without imposing or suggesting a limit to it, nay, makes the cherishing of it a duty and a measure of the seemingly antagonistic duty, implying that, the more we love ourselves, the greater will be the amount of the good we do to others. His fundamental law for the social life stretches the uniting wire between these opposite poles, and transmits from each to the other the current of personal and social obligation, making duty interest, and interest duty. The precept, "Thou shalt love thy neighbor as thyself," is simply absurd, if the imagined antagonism is real. But if these two principles, in form mutually hostile, are in fact kindred and mutually convertible,

N

so that each does the other's work, it must be by means of springs and wheels which underlie them both and the whole fabric of society, and which are kept in perpetual tension and motion by an omnipresent providence. Either this coincidence of self-love and beneficence is a law of nature, or it is a contradiction in terms and an impossibility in action. Let us consider how far it is a law of nature.

Look, first, at international relations. Unenlightened national self-love dictates war on the most trivial pretexts, quick resentment, prompt revenge, bold aggression, the preying of the strong upon the feeble. But if history has taught any lesson, it has taught the inexpediency and folly of needless war, even when most successful, and the expediency of peace at all sacrifices, and of mutual good offices among the nations. Nor has the lesson failed of reception. Though peculiar circumstances have led, within the lifetime of the present generation, to two of the greatest international wars on record, and though the grand police-movement of our government for the suppression and punishment of treason has assumed the form of a gigantic war, a change has already taken place in the policy of the civilized world. There have been numerous instances, of late years, in which controversies that half a century ago could have been settled only by armies have been adjusted by peaceful negotiation or arbitration; and it is distinctly seen on all hands that a generous, forbearing, long-suffering course in cases of international controversy is alone consistent with the welfare and progress of a state.

A similar change has taken place in the commercial relations of the civilized world. In the ignorant infancy of modern commerce the reigning doctrine was, that the surplus of the specie imported over that exported determined the balance of trade in favor of a nation, so that by any specific commercial arrangement one party must be the gainer, the other the loser. Thus the sole effort of diplomatists was to outwit one another, and to throw dust into one another's eyes; and as to mercantile matters, nations occupied a position of mutual antagonism, each looking for gain only at the expense of the other. This notion is now entirely exploded, and the principle is fully established, that between two nations no commercial arrangement can be advantageous to one party which is not so to both, that *virtual* reciprocity (which often differs widely, as in some instances our country has learned to its cost, from *literal* reciprocity) is the true basis of treaties, and that the enhanced prosperity of any one of the family of nations only offers an enlarged market for the industry and an expanded scope for the commerce of every other. Thus, though commerce seems an intensely selfish transaction, it is now girdling the earth with the zone of common interest, mutual good-will, and reciprocal helpfulness.

Among members of the same community I know of nothing that illustrates the concurrent tendency and harmonious working of self-love and mutual benevolence so strongly and beautifully as the system of insurance. At first thought, the appeal to the self-love of the uninjured as a resource against calamity might seem the height of absurdity, and the inscription, "Bear ye one another's burdens," placed over the office of a joint-stock company, might look like bitter irony. Yet what but such an appeal is the advertisement of an insurance company? What more fitting motto could an insurance office bear? This method of selfish benevolence, of philanthropic self-love, is already applied to the risks of fire, storm, and shipwreck, of sickness and death, and the extension of it to debts, contracts, suretyships, and other transactions in which a crushingly heavy burden is often thrown upon an individual, has been hopefully projected, so that in due time every calamity which can have its force broken by division will be thus dispersed by the beneficent working of pure self-love, — by a system into which no man enters except for his own benefit, yet into which no man can enter without becoming a public benefactor. This kindly agency, by which disasters that would overwhelm and ruin the individual are drawn off and scattered over a whole community with a pressure which none can seriously feel, might remind one of what takes place in a thunder-storm, when every twig of every tree and every angle of every moistened roof helps to lead harmlessly to the ground the electric force which, discharged at any one point, would deal desolation and death.

We may trace this same harmony between self-love and benevolence in the relations and intercourse of ordinary life. We have heard a great deal at times — I think that the phraseology has grown obsolete now, but it was rife when the Carlylese *patois* used to be spoken in cultivated circles — about whole men, and the necessity of every man's being a whole man, in himself complete, self-sufficing, and independent. There never was such a man, and never will be; and were there such a man, he would be as fair a specimen of humanity as one would be as to his physical nature who lacked hands, or feet, or even head. We are by nature the complements of one another. We cannot help leaning and depending on one another. We are like trees in a forest, each sheltered and fostered by its neighbor-trees, and liable to speedy blighting when transplanted to a solitary exposure. Our social natures are as truly a part of themselves as our physical natures; our affections, as our appetites; our domestic and civil relations, as our subjection to the laws of matter and of mind. The man whom we term selfish consults the needs of only an insignificant fraction of himself. The self-seeker (so called) leads a life of perpetual self-sacrifice and self-denial. He alone who benefits his neighbor does well for himself. He alone who does good gets good. He alone who makes the world the happier and the better by his living in it, becomes happier and better by living in it.

Thus we see that in the essential constitution of nations, communities, and the individual soul, self-love and mutual benevolence, so far from being antagonistic principles, are in perfect harmony, verifying the words of St. Paul, "The members, being many, are one body; and whether one member suffer, all the members suffer with it, or one member be honored, all the members rejoice with it."

You will not misunderstand me with reference to this matter. I by no means represent selfishness as a motive to benevolence; nor are those outwardly kind acts which are performed at the bidding of selfishness to be regarded as benevolent. Yet the highest benevolence is the highest self-love. Let me take a case familiar no doubt to some of my hearers, that of the missionary Boardman, and let me trace rapidly his career. He leaves the most flattering prospects near his native home. He crosses more than half the globe to toil for a race which proffers no hold on his æsthetic sensibilities, but whose only claim is its ignorance and wretchedness. He seeks out scattered hamlets in the almost impenetrable jungles and mountain-clefts of Burmah, and crosses swollen torrents, arid wastes, and rocky passes hardly trodden but by beasts of prey. His vigorous frame yields to perpetual and unresting labor. The hectic flush of approaching death deepens day by day, but he pauses not on his errands of mercy. His limbs refuse their office; still, "borne of four," like the paralytic in the Gospel, he carries from village to village the message of redeeming love. With the last sands of his life there is still a distant group of converted savages waiting to be baptized into the Christian fold, and through incredible fatigue he presses on to meet them. He presides at the service, welcomes the proselytes to his own blessed faith, pours forth for them his fervent exhortations and the prayers so soon to be merged in the worship of the heavenly temple. He dies conqueror on the bloodless field, the laurels of man's noblest victory crowning his fevered brow, and encircling his memory with a glory that time can never efface. Now in all this there was no self-renunciation, but an enlarged and enlightened self-love, — the love of a self complete and perfect, — of a self in those relations with universal humanity for which we are all created and destined, — of the immortal self which seizes its heavenly birthright, which knows the steps by which it is to mount on high, which cannot be content with any inferior and transient good while the supreme and everlasting good is within its reach.

My argument is this: I am attempting to illustrate the identity of Christianity with the religion of nature, and thus to prove that Christianity can have had no other author than the Author of nature. Nations, communities, individual men, only in these latter days are beginning to perceive the coincidence of self-love with benevolence, of the individual good with the general good. So far as observation and reasoning are concerned, it is wholly a discovery of modern times; but it is a discovery of what always was and must ever be, — of what lies in the essential constitution of human nature and society. Far back in barbarous antiquity this coincidence is dimly and partially shadowed in the Pentateuch. In the teachings of Jesus Christ it is made the basis of social morality, and underlies his entire code of duty between man and man. So many centuries before human philosophy and conscious experience began to verify this truth, it can have been derived only by revelation from Him who knew from the beginning what is in man.

LECTURE XI.

THE NATURAL RELIGION OF THE STATE.

As my course approaches its termination, I am oppressed by the multitude of topics that claim our attention, or would reward our inquiry. Among these I have chosen for the present Lecture the Natural Religion of the State, — of government, of man's political relations. In pursuance of the plan which I announced in my first Lecture, and have kept steadily in view, I shall attempt to legitimate on grounds of natural right the foundation-principles of political society propounded by revelation. In announcing the subject of this evening, I can hardly need to say that I am among those who find in the Bible not only the way out of this world, but the way in it, — not only preparation for a higher sphere of being, but the principles on which alone individual, domestic, social, and national life can be so ordered upon the earth as to secure the maximum of benefit and happiness.

It is among the discoveries of modern botanists, that the plant is built up solely by the multiplication of primitive cells, which contain in their microscopic proportions the characteristic properties of the completed organism. With reference to human society a similar discovery was announced in the Decalogue, and confirmed by Jesus Christ. I refer to the precept, " Honor thy father and thy mother, that thy days may be long in the land which the Lord thy God giveth thee." This last clause, a moment's examination will show you, is not the promise of a long life to a good son, but of long national life to a nation of good sons. The Decalogue is addressed to the people taken collectively, — "Hear, O Israel"; and this precept denotes, "Do you, as a people, cultivate filial reverence and piety, that you may long live in prosperity in your land." The command in itself is not strange; but the announcement in connection with it of so recondite, yet so essential a maxim of political philosophy, — a truth fundamental indeed, yet hardly recognized even now, — indicates a wisdom far beyond that rude age and people, and certainly gives no slight color of probability to the belief that God spake those words which have come down to us as the law given on Mount Sinai. Here then is the foundation-truth of the politico-religious system of the Bible. Let us see how far it is verified in the experience of mankind.

The state is but an aggregation of smaller communities; and they are but aggregations of the little groups of human beings that dwell in separate homes. The true organization of the state is analogous to that of the family. The administration of both is in theory alike paternal; its ends are protection and order. The duties of the citizen correspond to those of the child. They are submission and obedience, with no other limits than those which should restrain the child, namely, the carefully considered voice of conscience and the express law of God. The child may not commit theft or utter falsehood at the parent's command; but within the entire range of things not absolutely wrong he is bound to obedience, however unpalatable or irksome. In like manner, the citizen may not commit what he knows to be morally wrong at the bidding of the state; but there is no extent to which, within the limits of the right, he is not bound to act in opposition to his own wish, judgment, and interest, for the sake of loyalty to the government and order in the state. Nay, more, as the child, if his conscience will not let him obey his parent, is bound to yield to the penalty of disobedience, and to honor by his submission and suffering the parental authority whose command conflicts for the moment with a higher obligation, so the only safe rule for the citizen inhibited by an enlightened conscience from complying with the requisition of the state is for him to accept its penalty, — a rule commended to us by apostolic example, and by the sacrifice and suffering of the all-perfect Saviour.

Nor is our strictly filial relation to government modified by republican institutions, under which each man holds a portion of the sovereignty. The free citizen's acts of sovereignty are few, simple, and definite. They are confined to his exercise of the right of suffrage, his appropriation of the means requisite to enable him to exercise that right intelligently, and his free expression of opinion as to public men and measures. In everything else he is as much a subject bound to implicit obedience as if he were under a despotism. True, it demands a peculiarly clear moral discernment and active moral sense for one to be alternately sovereign and subject, — parent and child in the great national family. Therefore, for the citizens of a republic is the filial piety enjoined in the commandment I have cited pre-eminently the natural religion of the state; for citizens will be for the most part what they have been trained to be as children. You probably never knew a demagogue, a factious, brawling politician, one who despised laws and loved to defame rulers, who was not a stubborn son, a weariness to his father, and a perpetual grief to his mother.

Our Puritan ancestors and the colonists from the Old World in general brought to our shores the ancient notions of rigid family discipline. Unquestioning obedience was the law and the habit of their households. Wayward children fared worse with the early magistrates of New England than the majority of thieves and murderers fare now; for filial contumacy or irreverence was then regarded as " an iniquity to be punished by the judges." Thence sprang that pervading spirit of order, which in the last century survived the breaking up of old institutions, which for the most part quietly awaited the formation of our State and national governments, and then peacefully transferred its former allegiance to the newly constituted authorities. It was home-born habits alone that kept the nation out of the whirlpool of anarchy during the Revolutionary conflict, when the State governments really had very little power, nay, an existence so precarious that any extensive outbreaking of the mob-spirit would have crushed them. And had not the soldiers of the Revolution been for the most part trained in well-ordered families, they never would have laid down their arms, unpaid except in what they deemed worthless paper, but would have levied their hard-earned wages on the goods of the unarmed, and, not suffering themselves to be foiled by the impregnable virtue of their commander-in-chief, would have elevated some unscrupulous soldier of fortune to the headship of a military despotism.

The condition of things has sadly changed within the lifetime of the present generation. Laws have been perpetually nullified. Our legislative halls have often witnessed outrages that would disgrace an arena of prize-fighters. Mobs have not infrequently taken the law into their own hands, and have been abetted in their violence by men of conspicuous social and political standing. And am I not justified in saying that such disorders have sprung from lax domestic discipline, — from homes where children have borne sway, and their parents have served them? It was homes organized and governed after the divinely prescribed pattern that alone made a republic possible on this Western Continent; and if the old domestic *régime* is to be permanently reversed, if the elder are to serve the younger, if the whims of childhood and the caprices of youth, instead of the wisdom of mature experience, are to govern our families, the days of our republic are numbered, and are drawing to a close. Undisciplined homes will throw the state into anarchy; and the world will have to wait for a successful republican experiment till there shall be a nation that obeys the precept, and can claim the promise, of the fifth commandment of the Decalogue.

In this connection permit me to say a word of the present rebellion. The conflict is not between government and government, but between anarchy and order. Slavery, its salient cause, inflicts no evil so great as in subverting the natural order of the family, — in making children despots at the very age when they should be learning lessons of submission and obedience. A slaveholding population cannot be the nursery of good subjects. The present outbreak had its preparation and prophecy, first, in domestic insubordination, then and thence in those habits of private revenge and lawless violence which were sapping the foundations of society, and which have only reached their necessary and legitimate issue in a war aimed nominally against the authority of the United States, but virtually against the fundamental principles of all government and all social order.

To recapitulate what has been said, government and social order are a necessity of communities and nations. God has provided for the existence of government and order in the essential and natural duties, in the primal and natural law, of the filial relation, under which every child that obeys the very instinct of a child's nature becomes of necessity a loyal and orderly subject. Far back in the very rudest antiquity, — long before men could have begun to philosophize on their relations or on the analogy between the family and the state, — we find this fundamental, vital law of the state promulgated in a commandment that purports to have come directly from God. Can we resist the belief, that the announcement of a truth so manifestly beyond the age and people in which we find it was actually made by Him?

But while filial obedience alone can train worthy subjects for the state, there are yet other aspects in which government depends on the home-life, and is sustained by the family relation, so that, for a homeless community, anarchy or despotism would be the alternative. To an incalculable degree the home-instinct supplies the place of law, supersedes the harsher ministries of government, prevents crime, anticipates want, divides and lightens burdens which else no public organization could bear. The gravitation toward home is in every nation a stronger force than its police and armies are or can be, and accomplishes many purposes of prime importance which they could in no way fulfil. The few homeless members of a community are of immeasurably more charge, burden, and peril to its constituted authorities, than the overwhelming majority that have homes.

I called the tendency to domestic life the *home-instinct;*

for it is not the result of reason, or a choice from interested motives, and it has the same kind of power over the human will that the migratory instinct exerts upon the wings of a bird. When we look at the matter abstractly, homes are not necessary. We can conceive of life as existing independently of them. The conjugal and parental relations might be owned and kept sacred in the gregarious life which the socialists would have us lead. It has been, also, plausibly — though, I think, not without a latent sophistry — maintained, and is pretty generally believed, that, under a socialistic *régime*, there would be not only a more equable distribution, but a more profuse creation, of the elements of material comfort and enjoyment than under the institution of separate families. Yet under all forms and degrees of culture there is this irresistible tendency to a separate abode for each several family, — a latent consciousness, almost universal, that home can be surrendered only at an inconceivable sacrifice of all that is most loved and enjoyed.

By this instinct man is brought into analogy with the entire system of the universe. In the outward creation every object is at once a centre and a satellite. The sun, with circling worlds revolving around it, itself revolves around a centre of unnumbered systems. The planets, secondaries to the sun, are primaries to their moons. Every existence, every particle of matter, itself drawn by mighty attractions, is equally a centre of attractive force to surrounding objects. In human society almost all are moving in circumferences around distant centres, — all are so when compared in importance and dignity with the Supreme Being. But in his home every human being is himself a centre, — the parent, of reverence; the child, of love; the dependent, of tender care. Here the little become great, the obscure are clothed with honor. Those made to feel their insignificance everywhere else are important here. Those whose out-of-door life seems a blank have here a life on which others hang with interest. Each is here looked upon, in some measure, with a distinguishing regard, and all that there is in him or of him is held at its full value.

Cast your eye over a miscellaneous street group in some portion of your city not considered as peculiarly genteel. You see there many of no note in the world's esteem, cumberers of the ground, burdens on reluctant charity, drones in the great hive, pestilential elements in the lower strata of society. Yet there is one spot — mean and rude it may be — where the most squalid of that group is held in regard, perhaps in the same devoted affection that renders our homes happy. There is a wife, who has made her slender preparations for his evening comfort. There are children, who greet him by the most endearing of names, and who would not forsake his guardianship for the most affluent abode. He is a prince in his little empire, and its security and love make large amends to him for the toil and buffeting of his despised walk among men. Is he vicious, nay, a very Ishmael in his vices, his hand against every man and every man's hand against him? Still there are those here who will cover his failings, temporize with his infirmities, remember fondly his better days, and never yield up the long-deferred hope of better days to come. Is the dwelling the abode of common vices and of mutual strife? Still it is not always so. There are seasons of reconciliation, confidence, enjoyment, hope. Their journey through the desert brings them now and then to an oasis, though it be of scanty green and brief blossoming.

Look, again, at a cluster of children in some poor neighborhood. You will see those in whom, with the kindest heart, you cannot feel an individual interest, — the stupid, the ill-mannered, the squalidly apparelled, the misshapen. Yet among them all you may not mark a single unhappy face, and the most ragged and uncouth may have no more in look or manner to excite your pity than the best-conditioned. And why? Each of them has a home, and to him it has all the elements of a home. Each of them has a close and dear place in the hearts of one little circle. On that coarse and patched garment the mother has toiled lovingly, and has appended to it some hoarded remnant of obsolete finery, and to her eye it is not uncomely. The stupidity of this child is regarded at home as a prematurely meek and quiet spirit; the boisterous rudeness of that child as the exuberance of innocent mirthfulness. The deformed boy has a little sister who thinks him beautiful, and in all domestic arrangements and festivities his is the sunny side, the Benjamin's portion.

I have said enough for my purpose, which is to illustrate, not the blessedness of home, but its connection with the security and permanence of political institutions, — its agency in extending protection, care, and comfort to whole classes of persons, who else would be an unmanageable burden on the institutions of society, an intolerable, turbulent, and pestilential mass of pauperism and crime.

The malign action of whatever impairs the sacredness of home may be seen in the history of the decline and fall of the Roman empire. In the best days of the Republic the standard of domestic virtue was singularly pure and high for a heathen nation,[1] and the state drew health,

---

[1] "Repudium inter uxorem et virum, a condita urbe usque ad vicesimum et quingentesimum annum nullum intercessit." — Valerius Maximus, II. 1, § 4

vigor, and culminating power from frugal and well-ordered homes. In the time of the earlier Emperors the home-life of Rome in its profligacy distances description, and but for accumulated evidence would transcend belief. The facility of divorce left the wife not a day's security in her own dwelling,[1] and abandoned her children to a succession of step-mothers, whose very name became hateful from its identification with all fiendish forms of malice and cruelty. The father oftener bequeathed his estate to the last intriguing woman who had gained ascendency over his dotage, or to some sycophantic legacy-hunter,

[1] It will not be forgotten here that Cicero, whose standard of morality was by no means low for his time, repudiated his wife Terentia to marry a rich heiress, his own ward, and this, as his confidential and devotedly attached freedman Tiro asserted, in order to obtain means to pay his debts; and that he shortly afterward repudiated this new wife because she did not sympathize with him in grief for the death of his daughter. In like manner, Paulus Æmilius — certainly a man of rare merit — repudiated his young and virtuous wife for no assigned or known cause, simply saying, "My shoes are new, and well made, yet I must change them; but none of you can tell where they pinch me." Divorces *bona gratia, sine ulla querela*, and *sine causa* are referred to familiarly, as of every-day occurrence; and the *divortium bona gratia* is recognized as legal in the Pandect. Wives in process of time assumed, by general consent, and without legal hinderance, the same freedom from permanent matrimonial bonds which had been conceded to husbands. In attestation of this, it may be sufficient to cite the following well-known passage from Seneca: "Numquid jam ulla repudio erubescit, postquam illustres quædam ac nobiles feminæ, non consulum *numero*, sed *maritorum, annos suos computant?* et exeunt matrimonii causa, nubunt repudii? Tam diu illud timebatur, quam diu rarum erat; quia vero nulla sine divortio acta sunt, quod sæpe audiebant, facere didicerunt." — *De Beneficiis*, III. 16.

This subject is ably treated by Troplong, *De l'Influence du Christianisme sur le Droit Civil des Romains*. Troplong's treatise, otherwise admirable, evinces an occasional carelessness in the use of citations from classical authorities. Thus he writes (p. 206), "Mécène était célèbre par ses mille mariages et ses divorces quotidiens," and quotes, concerning Mæcenas, two passages from Seneca, "Qui uxorem millies duxit," and "Quotidiana repudia," but neglects to add to the first of these citations, "quum unam habuerit." Mæcenas, though a gross sensualist, had but one wife, and Seneca refers to the daily quarrels and reconciliations between him and his wife.

than to his rightful heirs, who inherited nothing but his depravity. The foulest of now nameless vices ran riot in the dwellings of the rich, while the poor were fed mainly by largesses bestowed for their complicity in public crime, and were trained to ferocity by gladiatorial shows and by the conflicts of men with savage beasts. All manly attributes died out of the heart of the nation, which had as little capacity of being fitly governed as its worst tyrants had of discreet and virtuous rule. The bonds of society became, like those of the family, a rope of sand. The hordes of Northern barbarians, whose strength had been compacted by those very domestic virtues — rude, yet genuine — which the corrupt civilization of the Empire had destroyed, found a people already hopelessly disintegrated, and thus their easy prey.

Similar lessons come to us from the modern history of France. From the age of Louis XIV. to the fall of the monarchy, gross licentiousness, brutalizing the court of every sovereign but the last, had descended through all grades of society, had obliterated the sanctity and dissolved the bonds of domestic life, and produced a condition which might remind us of St. Paul's words in describing the Gentiles of his day, — "without natural affection." The atheistical philosophy of the eighteenth century struck the axe at the root of whatever lingering belief or principle remonstrated against abounding corruption. Thus were trained, energized, maddened, the high-priests of the guillotine, — the men at whose bidding murder became law, innocence crime, religion felony, the rivers torrents of blood.

In more recent times the atheistical element, still intolerant of the divine order of the household, has largely crystallized into socialism, has had the phalanstery for its seminary, and the phalanx for its army of propagandism; and in the later French revolutions every one knows how prominent and decisive a part has been borne by socialism, which has repeatedly heaved society from its base, and threatened to whelm the nation in formless anarchy. In England and in our own country, — thanks to the Anglo-Saxon element of common sense, and, still more, thanks to the large infusion of Christian faith and principle, — the great experiments of socialism have been made chiefly on paper, and have cost only the printing; while the overt attempts to realize them have been too brief and of too limited extent to make their failure, or even their ephemeral existence, a matter of general notoriety.

Christianity attests its claim to be regarded as the religion of nature by cherishing, educating, and elevating the home-instinct. Alone of all religious systems, it fences the conjugal relation with inviolable sanctity. Its Founder recognized and honored the ties of kindred and of a common home. His presence blessed the marriage festival; his tears fell in sympathy with the bereaved household; and in his miracles he reunited broken families, and gave back the dead to the embrace of parents and of sisters. Wherever his religion is in the ascendant, in each little republic dwelling under the same roof are shaped in strength and beauty pillars of the state, on which the fabric of the public weal may rest securely, and may be built up into an ever closer conformity to the divine order of the heavenly commonwealth.

But the state needs more than stability. Stable as against misrule and anarchy, it should be so organized, governed, and energized, as to promote the progressive civilization of its members. To this progressive civilization, its hinderances from the sources usually regarded as its fountains, and its dependence for ultimate realization on certain principles of natural religion revealed and embodied in Christianity, I ask your attention in the remainder of this Lecture.

To *civilize* a man literally denotes to make him a citizen; that is, not merely to make him a voter who can be bribed, cajoled, or threatened to give a suffrage which has from his hand no more significance than it would have from the mouth of a dog, but to endow him with such traits of character and to environ him with such surroundings as shall enable him to enjoy all the privileges and to discharge all the duties of a citizen. The civilization of a people implies the multiplication of such citizens, — the extension of such traits of character and such privileges to the greatest possible number. Now in this sense there is no civilized nation upon the earth. In our own State, which approaches as nearly to that standard as any portion of the world, there is probably cast every year as large a number of unintelligent and irresponsible votes, as of votes proceeding from men who know the importance and feel the solemnity of the act; and what multitudes have we, who stand in no relation of mutual benefit to surrounding society, who neither receive nor impart other than harmful influences, and who, though not ostracized by the law, are as veritable pariahs as if they were recognized as an inferior and unprivileged caste!

Among the reputed criteria and means of civilization I would first name the increase of national wealth. This, if not connected with a diffusion equally rapid, is detrimental to the progress of civilization. It is, however, the natural tendency of wealth to increase without diffusion. Accessions of wealth necessarily come first into the hands of capitalists, and chiefly into those of large capitalists; and if there be no active moral principle to produce a different result, capital by its increase and concentration gets a more absolute control over the labor-market, and can dictate its own terms to the laborer. Moreover, experience has shown (and there are intrinsic reasons for it which it would require more time than I have now at my command to state in full) that with the growth of national wealth the rate of profits declines; and this decline is fatal to smaller capitalists, distances them in the competition for gain, impoverishes them, and throws them back into the ranks of labor. Great Britain has become the richest country in the world, but has declined in whatever the general diffusion of wealth can contribute to civilization, in proportion as it has grown rich. The landed property of England and Scotland is owned by hardly more than one third of the number of proprietors that possessed the soil at the beginning of the present century. Small estates are fast becoming extinct, and tenancies are merged in sheep-walks that sustain and employ not a tithe of their former inhabitants, and in immense farms, on which the children of the former owners or occupants have sunk in part into serfdom, while still larger numbers of them have been driven to the manufacturing towns, where their labor is often compensated just above the starvation-point. Cottage fires have been extinguished by thousands, and the ejected peasantry are thrown into the labor-market, to reduce still lower, if possible, the pittance of the toiling masses, or to swell the constantly growing multitudes dependent on public alms, who have constituted in some years no less than one sixth part of the entire population. Now wealth must and will increase, and its growth is in itself an object of desire; for it is the potential means of added comfort and privilege to all classes and every member of society. Yet in order to make it the actual means of the general good, there must be a law of distribution, — a law which can never be arbitrarily enacted, but must be imposed, if imposed at all, by moral, spiritual forces.

Another alleged criterion and agent of civilization is industrial development by means of machinery and the division of labor. As I showed you in a former Lecture, this must ultimately redound to the benefit — to the improvement and elevation — of the laborer; but not in and of itself. Its immediate tendency is in the opposite direction. With the same amount of early culture and the same hours of labor, a man is less of a man in intelligence, range of ideas, and scope of activity, when he makes a twentieth part of a pin, than if he made the whole pin, — when he merely watches a set of spindles or mends a web, than if he took the wool or cotton home and brought the finished cloth to market. Improvements in machinery tend of themselves to make the operative less and less a discretionary agent, more and more a mere mechanical force; and from authentic testimony before the English Parliament we might hesitate whether to prefer the civilization of the Malays and Hottentots, or that of which some dark vestiges yet remain in the factories and collieries of Great Britain. Now these improvements are inevitable, and are destined to be of immeasurable value to all classes and conditions of people; yet not without a moral, spiritual direction, which shall secure the universal diffusion, not only of the comforts of life which they multiply and cheapen, but equally of the time which they save, of the leisure for nobler purposes than handcraft which God proffers to the whole race through the mechanical powers and scientific resources placed by his providence at their command.

National strength, in the common and belligerent acceptation of the term, is also a false criterion of civilization. Of nations considered as physical forces, that is the strongest in which the individual will has the least scope, — in which authority is centralized, and the people can be moved in masses. Armies represent a nation's brute strength, and, except in a cause that vitally concerns the whole people, armies can be best sustained and recruited where the people have the least self-respect, the scantiest means of livelihood, and the lowest standard of home-comfort. In our present rebellion, even with the strongest array of patriotic feeling on the side of the Constitution and the Union, the South, with its much smaller population, was long able to cope with the Northern States on nearly equal terms, and has yielded to our superior resources with a slowness which we could not have anticipated, solely because slavery, by impoverishing and degrading the immense majority of the white inhabitants, has furnished a preponderantly large supply of the materials of which armies are best constituted, — men whose nature it is to yield to strong wills, and to make of themselves a mere physical force in the hands of their leaders. The diffusion of political power undoubtedly impairs a nation's strength, whether for aggression or for defence ; but it tends of necessity to raise a people equally above the purpose of aggression and the need of defence. This diffused power, — the power of general intelligence, civic and personal virtue, and enlightened public opinion, — which is the result of moral causes alone, is at once the effect, the cause, and the criterion of progressive civilization.

Knowledge claims to be, but is not necessarily, a civilizing agent. When increased and not diffused, it only aggravates social inequality, and puts into the hands of the few advantages which they can employ against the many. Thus the Egyptian priests at a very early epoch had the monopoly of nearly all the science and knowledge of the world, and they were thereby enabled to play at will on the credulity of the people, and to extort wealth, power, and influence from their superstitious fears. In all modern history, there have been no institutions of learning so exclusive as the two great English Universities. Sustained by the accumulated gifts of many generations, yet till within the last six or eight years closed against all Dissenters, — virtually closed, too, against all except the sons or *protégés* of the rich and the noble (for their eleemosynary foundations receive beneficiaries chiefly through aristocratic nomination or influence), — they have cast a shadow broader than their light, have thrust back from the heights of knowledge more than they have helped to scale them, have widened the distance between those of patrician and those of plebeian birth, and thus have tended to perpetuate those glaring contrasts in society, the reduction of which is a prime aim and criterion of civilization. Knowledge is too vast a power, and too prolific a source of power, to be safely centralized or made exclusive property. It becomes a social blessing only when its avenues are freely opened, its facilities multiplied, its attainments placed within the reach of every determined, vigorous and persevering seeker.

This review of the reputed sources and means of civilization authorizes the assertion, that the process of civilization consists, not in the accumulation of any good or of all goods, but in the placing of all or of any within the reach of the great body of citizens. We now ask, What is the principle of diffusion on which the hope of the race must rely? Whence springs the desire to diffuse, the forethought of members of the body politic for one another, the will and effort to throw into a common stock any and every class of advantages, material, intellectual, and moral? It springs from the sentiment and spirit of universal brotherhood, — from the philanthropy which cannot have without imparting, which deems the unshared gift unblessed. Still more, this sentiment and spirit must have a religious basis in the great truths of the fatherhood of God and the immortality of man. These alone authenticate rights on the one hand, and establish duties on the other. There is no earthly claim which the straitened and depressed can proffer. There is no earthly force that can unclench the grasp of monopoly, dissolve the close corporation of exclusive privilege, and throw wide the avenues of competition for all who will enter the lists.

Equality of right and privilege is utterly impossible on anti-religious or non-religious ground. No matter how liberal the institutions of government may be in name, they are liberal in their working, and in the intent of their workers, only when they are pervaded and energized by a religious faith in God and heaven. On no other ground is there any reason why they should be liberal. Take away men's common parentage and common destiny, — lop off from the column of human existence its base and its capital, — you leave men with nothing in common, with no points of union or of sympathy. They diverge widely from very birth; they differ greatly from one another in the outside of existence; they come together only beyond the grave. If they are not traced from a common Father and to a common destiny, then these earthly differences are all in all, and they lay a fair and just foundation for the encroachments and extortions of the richer and stronger, and for the abject, brute-like submission of the poorer and weaker. Unless mankind be one family in origin and destiny, might is right, selfishness is duty; society has no bond, imposes no mutual obligations; and the whole community naturally and necessarily divides itself into the two great classes of the preying and the preyed upon.

The unbeliever, then, though he style himself a republican, is such a friend to republican institutions as Samson was to the congregated nobles of Philistia. His hands grasp the pillars of Freedom's temple, but it is to tear them from their base, and to bury the structure and its inmates in common ruin. France tried the experiment; and never in the history of the race were human rights so outrageously violated, freedom so utterly subverted, man so trampled upon by man, as in the name of liberty and equality during the first French Revolution. Those self-styled champions of popular rights, Danton, Marat, Robespierre, and their colleagues, so far transcended the tyranny and cruelty of earlier times, that, placed at their side, the most relentless tyrants (except those who were idiots or madmen, as some of the Roman Emperors seem to have been) might appear in the comparison with clean hands and with honest and generous hearts. Thus was France tossed in the whirlpool of democratic tyranny, till she deemed herself only too happy to escape from her hydra-headed despot to the unbounded power and sole mastery of a single absolute sovereign.

It was this same absence of the religious element that vitiated the ancient republics, commonly so called, which were in fact, and without exception, oppressive oligarchies, in which the caste-system was established as rigorously as it is now in Hindostan, with the exception that there was no indelible taint of blood to prevent members of a lower caste from rising by extraordinary genius or some rare conjuncture of favoring circumstances.

We have thus seen that the diffusive principle and the entire system of equal rights and mutual obligations rest on the Divine paternity and the immortality of man, which appertain most emphatically to the natural religion of the state. But these are truths of natural religion which are clearly discerned only in the light of revelation, or, rather, only in the person of Him who could say, " He that hath seen me, hath seen the Father," and in whose resurrection the eternal life is made manifest. In the precise proportion in which his words are not only repeated in the creeds, but incorporated into the life of nations, must there be the progressive realization of those truths pronounced in our Declaration of Independence to be self-evident, yet never self-evident except at a high stage of Christian culture; — "that all men are created equal; that they are endowed by their Creator with certain inalienable rights; that among these are life, liberty, and the pursuit of happiness; that to secure these rights governments are established, deriving their just powers from the consent of the governed."

If Christianity be thus identical with the natural religion of the state, and if its advancement must inevitably result in the progressive civilization of the race, we have an affirmative answer to the question of the permanence of modern civilization. Egypt, Persia, Greece, and Rome successively attained a very high degree of civilization and refinement, and were subsequently overswept by barbarism, leaving only records and ruins of their former renown; and the story of their decline was told by a crafty old Roman, who, walking in his garden with the treason-plotting magistrate of a rival city, struck off with his staff the heads of the tallest flowers in a bed of poppies, — thus hinting that, if a few chief heads of the people could be laid low, the state would topple and fall. What is miscalled ancient civilization shone only on the tallest heads, and in any civil commotion or barbarian inroad they fell at once; and the mass left behind, not having partaken in the civilization, could not perpetuate it. Modern civilization must escape this fate by its universal diffusion, — by its having its shrine in the workshop no less than in the drawing-room, in the hamlet no less than in the metropolis. It must have for its defenders, not a chosen host, fit champions though few, but a national guard, a militia in which there are no exempts, in which every name is enrolled, and every laborer does battle for his soil. Such a civilization can die out only with the race. It must live, because Christianity, its mother, will ever live. It must grow, because her star will culminate. It must become universal; for the word of the Eternal has gone forth that her sceptre shall rule over all.

LECTURE XII.

THE SABBATH A LAW OF NATURAL RELIGION. — CONCLUSION.

In previous Lectures I have attempted to show the identity of the doctrines and ethics of Christianity with the religion of nature. Christianity has, also, its institutions, — *positive* institutions, as they are sometimes called, and so called from the general belief that there is no intrinsic reason for them, that they are wholly of arbitrary appointment, and that they might have had a different form and yet have equally answered their purpose. There is so little of formal institution or ritual belonging exclusively to Christianity, and what there is, though sacred and important, holds so secondary a place, that we might admit it to be arbitrary, and yet the admission would hardly modify our general view of the religion. But its few forms are not rigid and arbitrary. Its ceremonial hardly merits the name, so simple is it, so flexible, and so capable of variation in its details; while it is so significant, and so natural in its significance, that it easily ranges itself with doctrine and duty under the religion of nature, — and the more so, as it does not even draw its meaning from the historical facts of the Gospel, but rather from the fundamental and eternal laws which the Gospel reveals. Baptism, the initiatory rite, avails itself of the universally accepted symbol of purity; and even had it not been appointed by the authority of Christ, it might easily have come into use for the infant, whose native purity it typifies, while it prefigures the cleanness of heart and life which is our first hope and prayer for him in a world of temptation, and equally for the penitent, whose washing from sin is the one patent fact of his present state, and whose continued purity is at once his own fervent desire and the foremost wish of all who seek his true good. And were we left, without the request of Him whose redemption sacrifice this day[1] commemorates, to choose a rite which should express at once our thankfulness for the Divine benignity and our fellowship with our brethren still on the earth, with those who have passed on before us, and with the Lord of the living and the dead in whom the whole family in heaven and on earth is made one, what could we elect so natural, so appropriate, so fraught with associations at once of gratitude and communion, as the likeness of the social meal, crowned with the bounties of Providence, and in all times and lands refined and spiritualized by domestic love, friendly converse, and hospitable kindness? It was in the very simplicity of nature that He whose loving regards on the eve of his crucifixion passed down the vista of ages and comprehended unborn generations, sought for his commemorative rite no elaborate ceremony, but took bread and wine, the staff and the refreshment of daily life, and converted them into symbols of the deathless union of his spiritual family, — typifying still further the common duties, unostentatious sacrifices, daily wayside charities, which are the perpetual token, seal, and pledge of the communion of his disciples with one another and with their Lord and Master.

As regards the organization of the Church, it would ill become me to enter here on disputed ground; yet I

[1] This Lecture was delivered on the evening of Good Friday.

would beg leave to express my entire accordance with Archbishop Whately in the belief that no unvarying type of church-organization is expressly enjoined in the New Testament, or virtually prescribed by Christ or his Apostles, and that the absence of such a type shows it to have been the design of the Founder of our religion that each portion of the Church should adopt such interior arrangements as may best suit its needs, insure its stability, promote its edification, and extend its usefulness.

Omitting, for lack of time, the further treatment of the specifically Christian ritual, I pass to the consideration of the Sabbath, — an institution older than Christianity, yet so emphatically sanctioned by Jesus Christ, and so generally observed in his Church, as to be closely identified with his religion. The position which the Sabbath holds in the Decalogue claims our special attention. Of the ten commandments said to have been given on Mount Sinai, nine are confessedly not Hebrew, nor temporary, nor ritual, but of essential duty and universal obligation; presenting, in fine, an epitome of practical religion and ethics, from which you can take nothing without leaving a lacuna to be deprecated, to which you can add nothing that would not hold a secondary place as compared with either of the nine. With these, fourth in the series, preceded by the law which interdicts blasphemy, the most audacious of sins against the Majesty of heaven, and followed by the law which enjoins filial piety, the first and most sacred in the catalogue of relative duties and the fountain-head of all social virtues, stands the precept, "Remember the Sabbath day to keep it holy." If this be a mere provision of the Jewish ritual, why is it here, and not rather in Leviticus, along with the feast-days? Its place seems to indicate that it was regarded, at least by the author of the Pentateuch, as, like the rest, a law of natural right, intrinsic fitness, and universal obligation. Our Saviour and his Apostles evidently take this ground. They never represent the Hebrew ritual as binding on any but the posterity of Jacob, or as permanently binding on them; but they repeatedly cite the Decalogue as of universal and perpetual obligation, and Jesus quotes it in answer to the question, "What shall I do that I may inherit eternal life"? He also says, without limitation or qualification, "The Sabbath was made for man," — not for the Hebrews, but for all men; and in claiming as appropriate for its observance works of love and charity, he implies that there are other works, in themselves innocent and right, from which it is a duty to abstain on the Sabbath. Yet more, he cites God's beneficent activity during the age-long Sabbath of creation, whose seconds are centuries, as the precedent for his own beneficent activity on the weekly Sabbath, — "My Father worketh hitherto," that is, during the Sabbath that has supervened upon the successive epochs of creative energy, "and I work," that is, I in like manner do his work on the Sabbath that succeeds every six days of secular toil.

I cannot but regard the law of the Sabbath as a law of natural religion, revealed because it is natural, written on the tablet of stone because it had been first written on human, animal, and inanimate nature. It is as old as the creation, and the author of the Pentateuch did not antedate it when he made it coeval with the birth of man. We find repeated traces of it in Genesis, — in the division of time into weeks, and in the sacredness attached to the number seven in the lives of the ancient patriarchs. When mention is first made of the Sabbath in the history of the Israelites, prior to the giving of the law from Mount Sinai, it is named, not as a new institution, with the detailed exposition of reasons and motives which in the sacred books always accompanies important enactments made for the first time, but in precisely the way in which we should expect to read the re-enactment of an observance old, traditional, well known, yet partially disused during the season of Egyptian bondage;—"To-morrow is *the*[1] [a] rest of *the*[1] [a] holy Sabbath unto the Lord. Bake that which ye will bake, and seethe that which ye will seethe; and that which remaineth over, lay up for you to be kept until the morning." The septenary division of time from the earliest ages was uniformly observed all over the Eastern world. We find vestiges of it among the Egyptians, Assyrians, Persians, and Arabs, nations severed from the common ancestral tree long before the birth of the Hebrew commonwealth. The Greeks evidently brought with them from the East the septenary institutions, associations, and habits common to the Oriental nations; for both Hesiod and Homer speak of "the seventh, the sacred day."

The primeval origin of the Sabbath becomes the more probable when we consider that the week is not an astronomical division, but that it is precisely adapted to confuse and derange the month,—the most obvious astronomical period longer than the day. The epochs of the new and the full moon were prominently marked by all ancient nations. The average length of the month is twenty-nine and a half days, so that each successive festival of the new or the full moon must have recurred later in the week

---

[1] The article [the] is wanting in the Hebrew. Its presence would strengthen our argument; yet it is so often omitted by the Hebrew writers in positions in which modern usage would require the definite article, that no adverse inference can be founded on its absence.

than the preceding, — a fact which shows that the week is more likely to have been a primeval institution, than to have resulted from an awkward attempt to divide the month by a divisor which leaves with regard to the month an annoying and embarrassing remainder.

The law of the Sabbath is a law of the human body. Man's physical strength will not bear a perpetual strain. It has always been found necessary to give periods of relaxation to the toil-driven. Where the weekly Sabbath has not been so appropriated, its place has been supplied, though imperfectly, by festivals, public games, saturnalia, when the axe, the hammer, and the distaff have been laid aside, and the slave has been as free as his master. Regarding man simply as a mechanical agent, and considering the question how in a series of years he may be enabled to accomplish the most labor, ample experience has shown that six working-days in the week are worth more than seven. Where there are no regular intervals of repose, the laborer is soon broken down, and becomes a spiritless slave, incapable of half the effort and endurance which sit lightly on him who has one day of rest in seven. The farmer in hay-time and harvest-time, the merchant in a busy season, the hard-working mechanic, feels on Saturday night that he has used all his strength and energy, and can toil no longer. Did he rise the next morning to pursue his task, it would be with a heavy heart and a listless hand. But the day of rest passes over him, and he is renovated, and goes back to his labor with fresh vigor and an elastic spirit. The commandment, "Remember the Sabbath day," is written on every muscle and sinew in man's frame, and he who remembers not the Sabbath for its benign uses must remember it in lassitude and unprofitableness.

Moreover, experience has shown, not only that the weekly day of rest is needed, but that it suffices for industrial purposes. The maximum of health, strength, and working capacity is attained in those nations and communities where the weekly Sabbath is best observed, and the residue of the time devoted to the pursuits of active life, and from this maximum there is a falling off, equally, on the one hand, in communities and kinds of labor on which "Sunday shines no Sabbath day," and, on the other, in those countries in which numerous holy days have been converted into holidays,—a system which uniformly engenders idleness and unthrift.

The law of the Sabbath is written also on the constitution of the beasts that aid man in his labor; and the extension of its immunities to cattle in the Decalogue, in an age when neither humanity nor far-sighted selfishness could have had much place in their treatment, is one of the many internal evidences that this sublimest compend of practical ethics emanated from the careful Providence of Him who despises nothing that he has made. Before stage-coaches on our long routes of travel became historical, there was, in the economy of brute life, a contrast, the statistics of which, if not substantiated by the records of many years, would be almost incredible, between the lines on which coaches ran but six days in the week, and those on which the weekly Sabbath was not recognized. Chateaubriand says, that during the reign of atheism in France, when the National Assembly substituted for the week and the Sabbath the decimal division of time, with a holiday every tenth day, the peasantry in the rural districts found that their cattle would not forsake the law of God for the ordinance of man. The strength and animal spirits of the beasts declined under the new *régime*.

"Our cattle," said the rustics, "know the Sabbath, and will have it";[1] and the one day's rest in seven was resumed in many quarters on economical grounds, before the nation shook off the nightmare of infidelity.

The law of the Sabbath is written even on inanimate nature. The artificial aids and multipliers of human industry, the fixtures of steam and water-power, locomotive engines, the strongest and best-adjusted machinery, need periodical rest and refitting, no less than the limbs and sinews of the operative; and though we cannot assign to the repairing of water-courses and the cleansing of boilers an important office among the means of religious edification in a manufacturing city or village, yet the notorious fact that Sunday is thus employed, often from midnight to midnight, shows that cupidity driven to desperation can never obliterate the Sabbath.

In a former Lecture I illustrated the tendency that there is in the civilized world to over-production, leading to a glut in the markets, and necessitating the occasional suspension of many departments of industry, with loss of income to the capitalists and of subsistence to the laborers. It is obvious that six days' work in each community will more than suffice for the needs of the seven days; and the effect of the weekly Sabbath, supposing that seven days' labor would really produce more than six, (which I more than doubt,) is therefore not to deprive the community of the needful fruits of labor, but to check the injurious excess of production.

I have thus far spoken only of the physical necessity for the Sabbath. It is, if possible, even more absolutely essential to the human intellect. When the mind pursues

---

[1] "Nos bœufs connaissent le dimanche, et ne veulent pas travailler ce jour-là." — *Génie du Christianisme*, Partie 4ieme, Livre 1er, Chap. IV.

the same track from day to day without repose, either the mind itself loses its elasticity and its full working power, thus winning for itself unsought and unwelcome relief, or else the overtasking of the brain induces bodily disease and infirmity. But, with the weekly rest, or the change of occupation which is the most desirable mode of rest to the vigorous intellect, the most arduous pursuits of learning, science, or professional duty may be sustained through a long life with unflagging and unwearied energy. Should any one doubt the necessity of which I speak, I could only ask him to assume for a while the else easy and happy charge of the clerical profession, in which one is tempted, nay, often compelled, to devote all his days to the same class of duties, — the noblest, the most delightful, the most engrossing that can be devolved on man, — and then see how surely his mental vigor and animal spirits will droop after a few months of continuous toil, so that he must either replace his lost Sabbaths by a prolonged season of recreation, or bear the penalty in chronic illness and disablement. I doubt whether any clergyman can be found so hardy as not to have ascertained that the law of the Sabbath is a natural, constitutional law, and in that respect, if in no other, as old as the creation. The testimony of the greatest minds of modern times in this behalf is clear, full, and strong. I might easily fill my Lecture with citations from men whose names alone are solid arguments. But, not to multiply witnesses on a point so obvious and self-evident, I will barely quote a testimony uttered in my own hearing. The venerable Nathan Dane, to whom the country is indebted for the Ordinance of 1787 for the Government of the Northwest Territory, was deemed the most erudite lawyer of his time. He lived to the age of eighty-three, and for many years, and till within a few weeks of his death, he spent fourteen hours a day in his library. He seemed incapable of light labor or of literary recreation, and eighty-four hours of every week were given to the driest details of law, political science, and recondite history. Not long before his death, he told me that he attributed his prolonged and undiminished capacity of study to his having for a full half-century devoted the Sabbath to an entirely different class of studies from those which occupied him during the week, — not to easy religious reading (for he lacked the ability of even such relaxation), but to the Hebrew Scriptures in the original, to ecclesiastical history, and to the profounder themes of inquiry connected with the Christian revelation. "From Sundays thus spent," said he, "I have always returned on Monday morning to my week's work, refreshed and strengthened."

The Sabbath is also of incalculable worth as a civilizing agent. How little opportunity would there be for reflection, for the growth of meditative wisdom, for plans that look beyond the passing moment, in a community, where from the beginning to the end of the year there was an unbroken round of grovelling toil! It is this periodical change in the routine of life, this diversion of the thoughts into purer channels, that gives freshness and vigor to the general mind, imparts the impulse to improvement, and creates the leisure and cherishes the reflective habits which alone can make the experience of the past availing. It is the Sabbath that calls men's thoughts off from the working-day world to the region of the intellect and the imagination, to unearthly questionings and musings, to philosophy and poetry. Hence alone the popular taste and demand for literature. Hence the existence of an intellectual department of society, — of classes of men whose business it is to instruct, edify, and enrich the public mind. Were there no Sabbath, there would still be a literature; for the few master-spirits of the race would shine out with a radiance which surrounding darkness would be unable equally to comprehend and to quench. But these greater lights would beam as solitary stars. There could not be the galaxy of pure taste, refined sentiment, and elevated thought, in which Christendom now rejoices. The literature that sprang into being would be the property of the few, not of the many. The great mass of the people would never find leisure to grow conversant with it, except as it might assume the lyric form, and ally itself to music.

The distinction here suggested may be clearly traced between Hebrew and classic literature and civilization. The Old Testament constituted in the strictest sense a national literature, and all sorts and conditions of people were familiar with it. Hebrew civilization, too, though its culminating point was far below that of the Periclean or the Augustan age, yet penetrated the whole community, permeated every vein and artery of the body politic. The civilization of Greece and Rome, on the other hand, as I showed you in my last Lecture, was confined chiefly to the circles of rank and wealth, leaving the great body of the people unbenefited. In producing this contrast, the student of history must, I think, ascribe more influence than to all other causes combined to the fact that in Judæa the whole population had one day in seven sequestered from the dusty arena for calmer thoughts and more elevating duties, while upon Athens and Rome there rose no stated day of rest and devotion.

The Sabbath vindicates for itself still further a place in the religion of nature, on the ground of its domestic influences. The rust of the world would corrode the chain of home sympathy and love, were it not burnished in these frequent intervals of holy rest. Think of the lives which the great majority of men — the rich often more than the poor — lead during the six working-days, — so engrossed by labor or harassed by business as hardly to snatch a hasty meal with their families, frequently not even that, forth before the day has fairly opened, returning perhaps not till a late evening hour, rarely getting sight of the younger members of the household, and meeting the elder only at hurried moments or in extreme weariness. Were this the routine of the whole year's life, how could the members of a family become acquainted with one another's minds and characters? The same persons might for half a century call the same house their home, yet there would be no communion of soul with soul, no growth of common tastes and sentiments. The father would be the mere steward of his family, and the dwellers beneath his roof would be little more to him than pleasant fellow-lodgers at an inn. But the Sabbath has attached to home an interest and a worth which can be derived from no other source, has cherished and refined those invaluable departments of art and taste which have the comfort and adornment of home-life for their object, and stands second to none of the agencies by which are shed upon us the holy and benignant influences of Him in whom all the families of the earth are blessed.

The Sabbath is equally essential to man's political well-being, and especially to the permanence of free institutions. It is the day of equal rights. It levels all factitious distinctions. It owns no differences of wealth, or caste, or race, or color; but proffers its benediction to all alike. It recognizes man as he is in the counsels and providence of Him who is no respecter of persons. It at once humbles pride, and relieves depression. It promotes a healthful sympathy and a mutual interest among all classes of society. It commends the poor to the charity of the more prosperous, and numberless are the sources of succor for the burdened and the indigent which flow from the Sabbath assembly. There no privileged order steps before the rest, — no lordly pontiff distances and repels the humble worshipper; but as high and low, rich and poor, are brought into a community of relation with their Creator and Preserver, and through him with one another, they cease to be infatuated on the one hand, and disheartened on the other, by the various lots which Providence has assigned to them. Thus the spirit of exclusive aristocracy is repressed, while the tendency to agrarianism and communism is equally checked. The haughty separatist and the factious leveller are both rebuked, and the foundations of republicanism are laid in that essential equality before God which needs no outward addition to make itself perfect.

It is a striking confirmation of these views, that the friends of tyranny and of anarchy have manifested equal fear of the Sabbath, and in numerous instances have sought to undermine its obligation and to violate its sanctity, as a step of prime importance toward the subversion of freedom or of law. Thus, when the British crown was most active in its encroachments on the liberties of the people, the Sabbath was a chief point of attack, and edicts were issued from the court, and published from the desecrated pulpits of an Erastian and sycophantic church, instituting for the day of worship noisy, riotous, and brutalizing sports. We have seen that the same hostility to the Sabbath was manifested by the destructives of the French Revolution. In our own land and day, the radicals, levellers, and no-government men who from time to time have lifted their voices against law, wholesome subordination, and salutary restraint, have uniformly cast the first stone at the Sabbath, its institutions and their guardians.

The Sabbath proffers peculiar claims to be regarded in its political uses, in connection with the eager enterprise of a young and growing people. Our nation is, no doubt, characterized beyond all others by earnestness and haste in the pursuit of wealth and preferment. And if, in the midst of this breathless competition, everything sacred is not trampled under foot; if the character of our merchants is marked, with rare exceptions, by sterling integrity; if there be a surviving seed of true patriots, — all this is owing, not to Christianity, (for where would its counsels find entrance among the closely crowded cares and conflicts of daily life?) but to the Sabbath, which has called the merchant and the statesman to their homes and to their own hearts, has checked their ardor of pursuit, let in the solemn light of eternity on transient gain and honor, uttered words of duty and accountableness, and held up the infallible mirror of Divine revelation to the conscience and the life.

Then, again, in our frequently recurring seasons of fierce political excitement, who can say to what a height the embittered passions of partisans might mount, and in what desolating floods of uproar and violence they might discharge themselves, were it not for these merciful breathing-spells, when He who once held the pulse-beat of the Galilean sea calms the billows of human strife, and calls the stormy wrath of man to praise Him? On the six days men remember their grounds of animosity and conflict; on the seventh, those who have garrisoned opposite camps through the week meet face to face, kneel side by side, and thoughts of toleration and kindness break in upon their opinionativeness and mutual repugnancy. The voice comes to them, and forces itself upon their hearts, "All ye are brethren, — why fall ye out by the way? Why wrong ye one another?" And though the morrow renew the strife, they return to it with slackened interest, and with the hope, awakened by the period of hallowed calm, for the speedy close of the controversy, and the quiet reunion of the distracted body politic.

The Sabbath is the law of man's religious nature, being absolutely essential to the social expression, the diffusion, and the transmission of the religious sentiment. Public worship grows naturally and spontaneously from the great foundation-truths of a common paternity and a common destiny. These, once admitted and felt, imply and crave religious communion. But public worship and enlarged communion demand a Sabbath. The assembly cannot be convened unless the time be appointed and known beforehand, nor frequently gathered unless at stated intervals. For so solemn an act as Divine worship, it seems fitting that the same day be observed throughout a whole community, in order that business and amusement may not interfere with devotion, and that the worshippers may find nothing going on around them which shall call off their attention from their religious duties, or disturb and wound their sensibilities in performing them. Hence natural piety would prescribe for the stated days of worship such a degree of rest and such an air of solemnity in the community as may comport with the dignity of the service in which its devout members are engaged.

Yet again, were there no Sabbath, it is to be feared

that for the great mass of every community, nay, for many who through the form of worship have been suffused by its spirit and energized by its power, there would be no holy time. The Sabbath, by suspending worldly engagements, creates a void which there is always hope that devotion may come in and fill. How else could we get the ear of the indifferent for religious truth and duty? How could we induce them to pause long enough in the chase of present pleasure or gain, to think of the enduring wealth and honor of the Christian calling? You go to a man in the rush of business or the spring-tide of gayety, and he puts you off till "a more convenient season." On the Sabbath the convenient season has come. The world is still; the congregation is gathered, and he joins the multitude that keep holy time. He may go to scoff, he may go to criticise, he may go merely because others go;—still he is there, and the arrow of conviction may be driven home, and send him forth to repent and pray. These blessed days are

> "Wakeners of prayer in man; — his resting-bowers,
>   As on he journeys in the narrow way,
> Where, Eden-like, Jehovah's walking-hours
> Are waited for as in the cool of day; —
> Days fixed by God for intercourse with dust,
>   To raise our thoughts and purify our powers; —
> Periods appointed to renew our trust; —
>   A gleam of glory after six days' showers."

I have thus, I trust, vindicated the claim of the Sabbath to its place in the religion of nature. Permit me, in closing, to commend this primeval institution to your sacred reverence and your loyal observance. It has nurtured — and nowhere more than in our own New England — great and holy men, elect spirits in every walk in life, — those who have become chief by being servants of all, those who have irradiated the lowest stations by virtues that would have adorned the highest. The vast themes of religious contemplation to which the Sabbath invites us enlarge the matrices of thought, expand the framework of the soul, stretch the extensor muscles of the intellect, nerve and sharpen the apprehensive powers, feed and exalt the imagination, and re-create the soul in an ever-closer likeness to the all-creative Spirit. He who, like Jacob with the angel, wrestles in these hallowed hours with truths vast as the universe and boundless as eternity, gets the reward of the athlete in comprehensive grasp and cogent force of intellect, and can thus become adequate in every field to cope with the noblest minds, to wrest her secrets from Nature, its hoarded wealth of beauty from poetry, its power to enlighten, guide, and gladden from every form of literature and art.

Above all, let the Sabbath be prized and honored for the sake of the spiritual nature. The religious life may, indeed, derive light and warmth from the few moments of daily devotion, — from holy thoughts that rise in the midst of toil and care. But these need their prolonged kindling seasons, and I have yet to learn that daily devotion or the prayer without ceasing can be well sustained without the agency of the consecrated Sabbath. On other days there are numerous influences unfavorable to the spirit of piety, and the altar-flame must often be like a fire built on ice, the fuel brought from afar; and whence but from the Sabbath-pile? But if the soul gives itself up on that one day to religious thoughts, humane sympathies, peaceful contemplations, spiritual desires and affections, it takes with itself a treasury for the draft and waste of the working-day world, — bread of heaven that may nourish it for its six days' journey. "Make all days alike," is a maxim not unfrequently urged by those who hold the Sabbath in low esteem. I would echo it. Make all days alike, — the nearer alike the better. But level upward, not downward. Keep the delectable mountains, which God made when he made the world, which tower above the waters of the Deluge, and fill in the intervening valleys as high as you can. Let Sabbath thoughts and feelings flow down continually into the week-days, and leave their rich deposit there, to render the whole life purer, nobler, more faithful, more heavenly. Let the valleys rise higher and higher as the weeks roll on, till you have made all days alike, the ground all table-land, — till the life is a perpetual Sabbath, a prototype of the New Jerusalem Sabbath, whose sun goes not down, whose worship never dies upon the ear, of which it is written, "The glory of God doth lighten it, and the Lamb is the light thereof."

I have thus completed my assigned course of Lectures; but I feel that I have barely marked for you here and there a station of thought, and made with you fragmentary surveys which it remains for you to connect and extend by your own reflection and research. I commenced by showing you the necessary identity of natural and revealed religion, which differ, not in their substance, but in their sources. I set forth the insufficiency and inadequacy of our own powers for the attainment of religious truth. I exhibited revelation, miracles, and authoritative scriptures as postulates of natural religion, and therefore in themselves antecedently probable. I presented the evidence of the Divine paternity in nature and in human experience, and considered the more patent objections to it derived from suffering, from moral evil, and from the condition of the unprivileged portion of our race. I illustrated the Divine providence in human art, and in the distribution of capacities and endowments among men. I demonstrated the Divine holiness from the human conscience, and from the inevitable law of moral retribution. I exhibited the accordance of the official relations of Jesus Christ to mankind with natural religion. I adduced the extra-Scriptural arguments for the immortality brought to light in the Gospel. I illustrated the accordance of Christian morality with natural, universal, and eternal law, and the foundation in nature for the fundamental precepts of love to God and to man, and of personal and social duty. I considered the politico-religious basis of government and social order. Finally, in the present Lecture, I have shown that Christian institutions — the Sabbath especially — are not arbitrary, but legitimated on grounds of natural fitness.

I have endeavored, without transcending the theme assigned to me, — natural religion, — to present what seems to me the most important portion of the evidence for Christianity. But because I have laid emphatic stress on its coincidence with nature, I would not have you infer that I hold the external evidences on which also it relies in light esteem. On the other hand, they seem to me impregnable, and they have gained new strength with the researches of the present age in geography, in archæology, and especially in the disinterred monuments and deciphered records of Egypt and of Nineveh. But a first-hand acquaintance with these evidences requires time, which indeed cannot be more worthily spent, but which all have not at their command, and an extended familiarity with books to which few except those who devote themselves to theological study have easy access.

On the other hand, the proof of the Divine origin of Christianity derived from its accordance with man's nature and needs, and with the essential laws of the outward and the spiritual universe, can be appreciated by every serious mind, and to me it seems complete, demonstrative, unanswerable. In these two classes of evidences, God has given us in behalf of his revelation, as it were, two independent and amply competent witnesses, either worthy of entire credence, and both together creating an assurance beyond the reach of cavil or the shadow of doubt. But the argument from nature has one prerogative. External evidence and testimony prove that Christianity is a Divine revelation, but not that it is final and sufficient for all time. Its coincidence with nature demonstrates its eternity and its universal adaptation, and proves Christ not only the accredited Author, but equally the Finisher of the faith which alone can renovate, sanctify, and save our race.

If Christianity has its foundation in man's nature and needs, it can never be outgrown, nor can its records become obsolete. It is the sole Sun of righteousness, and must forever be the central orb of the spiritual universe. But it may or may not be our luminary and guide. As the earth in its annual circuit throws our northern zone where only the oblique rays of the winter solstice reach it, and vital warmth almost deserts it, so may we make for our souls a winter solstice by our worldliness, our contented sensualism, our voluntary guilt. And we may, too, create for ourselves a perpetual summer solstice by our earnest aspirations, by our docility of spirit, by hearts ever open to the influence of the Divine truth and love.

THE END.

www.ingramcontent.com/pod-product-compliance
Lightning Source LLC
Chambersburg PA
CBHW021358230426
43666CB00006B/565